Resisting the Devil

Resisting the Devil:

A Catholic Perspective on Deliverance

*A Bridge between Exorcism
and the Sacrament of Reconciliation*

By Neal Lozano

Our Sunday Visitor Publishing Division
Our Sunday Visitor, Inc.
Huntington, Indiana 46750

Nihil Obstat: Msgr. Michael Heintz, Ph.D., *Censor Librorum*
Imprimatur: ✠ John M. D'Arcy
Bishop of Fort Wayne-South Bend
May 29, 2009

The *Nihil Obstat* and *Imprimatur* are official declarations that a book or pamphlet is free of doctrinal or moral error. No implication is contained therein that those who have granted the *Nihil Obstat* or *Imprimatur* agree with the contents, opinions, or statements expressed.

Except where otherwise noted, Scripture citations used in this work are taken from the *Catholic Edition of the Revised Standard Version of the Bible (RSV)*, copyright © 1965 and 1966 by the Division of Christian Education of the National Council of the Churches of Christ in the United States of America. Used by permission. All rights reserved.

English translation of the *Catechism of the Catholic Church for the United States of America* copyright © 1994, United States Catholic Conference, Inc. — Libreria Editrice Vaticana. English translation of the *Catechism of the Catholic Church: Modifications from the Editio Typica* copyright © 1997, United States Catholic Conference, Inc. — Libreria Editrice Vaticana.

English translations of Vatican documents are from the Vatican Web site, www.vatican.va.

Every reasonable effort has been made to determine copyright holders of excerpted materials and to secure permissions as needed. If any copyrighted materials have been inadvertently used in this work without proper credit being given in one form or another, please notify Our Sunday Visitor in writing so that future printings of this work may be corrected accordingly.

ISBN: 978-1-59276-709-0 (Inventory No. T1030)
LCCN: 2009941611

Cover design by Tyler Ottinger / Cover photo: Jupiter Images
Interior design by Siok-Tin Sodbinow

PRINTED IN THE UNITED STATES OF AMERICA

Endorsements for Neal Lozano, *Resisting the Devil*

I am convinced that this book, and the model of deliverance prayer that it describes, are of tremendous importance for the new evangelization. Neal Lozano is one of the pioneers of an approach to deliverance prayer that is simple yet effective, pastorally sound, and fully integrated into the sacramental life of the Church. He shows how this form of prayer, rooted in the New Testament, is a powerful way to experience, and help others experience, the full freedom that Jesus came to give us.

— Dr. Mary Healy, author of *The Gospel of Mark*,
Catholic Commentary on Sacred Scripture

Neal Lozano's book *Resisting the Devil* is an extremely important work. By bringing a Catholic perspective to this aspect of Church life he has placed our conflicts with evil spirits within the great tradition of Christian spirituality ranging from the early Church to our modern awareness of psychology. Not only can this common sense work establish the need and the nature of deliverance, but it also places deliverance once again as a dimension, in one form or another, of every serious Christian life. I would hope that every spiritual director and counselor will read this study and deepen their practice of this ministry of mercy.

— Fr. Francis Martin, Professor of New Testament, Dominican
House of Studies, Washington, DC

Finally, a thoughtful work that facilitates a balanced dialogue between deliverance ministry and the Church's rite of exorcism. I warmly recommend this book to anyone journeying with individuals variously afflicted by the Evil One.

— Fr. Jeffrey Grob, JCD/PhD, Pastor, Canonist

As a retired bishop who served in episcopal ministry for thirty years, I welcome Neal Lozano's book, *Resisting the Devil*. Over the years, I experienced both the need for the ministry of exorcism and deliverance and the lack of ministers capable and willing to exercise these ministries not because of a lack of good will, but rather because of a lack of understanding and formation.

Lozano's book is a valuable contribution to the growing body of literature on these ministries, and as such responds to a long-standing, current, and serious need in the life of the Church.

— Most Rev. Adam Exner, OMI,
Archbishop Emeritus of Vancouver, Canada

Resisting the Devil is a must-read for all those involved in pastoral ministry, spiritual direction, and for those who administer the Sacrament of Reconciliation. His work enlightens the reader to the great need for deliverance ministry among God's people and discovering the gift of "freedom" found in Jesus Christ.

— Msgr. Myron Cotta, Vicar General,
Diocese of Fresno, CA

Neal Lozano has written a marvelous book which will be extremely helpful in the most difficult part of any exorcism or deliverance process, namely, discernment. He has given us a way to wade through some of the most difficult problems in the field of spiritual healing, and for that I am very grateful. I would recommend it to anyone!"

— Fr. Thomas J. Euteneuer, Exorcist and President,
Human Life International

The Lord has given Neal Lozano wisdom and compassion for those many Catholics who while trying to live their faith, experience pain, emptiness, bondage and confusion. For decades he has served people who need to experience the Father's healing love and the freedom that Christ and His Spirit can bring. Neal is a brave and compassionate pioneer whose motivation is to heal the wounds of sin and free the afflicted from the influence of the demonic. His new book, based on a well-considered theological understanding and broad pastoral experience, is a significant contribution to making this wisdom available to the wider Church.

— Ralph Martin, author of *The Fulfillment of All Desire: A Guidebook for the Journey to God Based on the Wisdom of the Saints*

In *Resisting the Devil,* Lozano targets his own Roman Catholic tradition with his message of a general, church-wide, lay ministry of deliverance. And it is this very focus that makes this book uniquely valuable to Protestant beneficiaries of Neal's ecumenical ministry. Neal patiently relates the general "charism of deliverance" to the Church's official Rite of Exorcism and the Sacrament of Reconciliation, on the one hand, and to New Testament data on the other. Thus, he treats Protestant readers to a broader historical perspective, schooled in some important distinctions, and once again challenged by the comprehensive grace of God revealed in the gospel of Jesus Christ. This is a valuable complement to Neal's *Unbound: a Practical Guide to Deliverance.*

— Stephen S. Taylor, Associate Professor of New Testament, Biblical Theological Seminary

With each passing year since I first learned about deliverance from Neal Lozano in 2002, I become more convinced that it is a missing key to healing in those many patients who just don't seem to get much better with counseling and medication alone. The reason may be that Medicine and Psychology do not, generally, conceive of man in his totality and do not make an account — directly — for the effects of sin and evil on his condition. Most importantly to me, Neal's Unbound Model is a wonderfully simple guide to help believers get in touch with their true self and then to apply the healing power of forgiveness and renunciation in daily life. I have seen firsthand how Neal's approach to deliverance has brought hope to many by offering truth to them in a loving, effective way. I highly recommend *Resisting the Devil* to anyone who longs to walk freely his rightful inheritance, the abundant life promised to those who believe in and respond to the central message of Jesus Christ."

— Edward McGonigle, MD, psychiatrist

Neal Lozano in his book *Resisting the Devil* examines in a very practical way the devil, deliverance and exorcism today. He gives us a way that people can be really free to live their lives as sons and daughters of God. I have used the book's Unbound Model in my diocese with success in healing and delivering people caught up in sinful acts. I recommend *Resisting the Devil* as an essential reading for priests, pastors, lay leaders and also for Christians who want a fresh and practical insight into deliverance today.

— Bishop Anthony Burgess, Diocese of Wewak,
Papua New Guinea

Contents

CHAPTER I

Exorcism and Deliverance: Two Paths to Spiritual Freedom for Catholics

For freedom Christ has set us free.

— Gal 5:1

One in five young adults suffers from a personality disorder strong enough to be considered mental illness.[1] That piece of information, as startling as it is, was reported by the Associated Press in December of 2008 and disseminated widely in American newspapers. Several weeks before I read that troubling statistic, my local public radio station broadcast an interview with a German psychologist, practicing in England, who explained that many young people in both Germany and England continue to suffer from the trauma of World War I and World War II.[2] The First World War ended 90 years ago, yet here was a professional man whose practice and research had shown him that the effects of war trauma had passed down through the generations and resulted today in an epidemic of mental illness.

With such large numbers involved, we can assume that many Catholics are among those who are emotionally and psychologically troubled. Yet St. Paul tells us clearly that Christ has set us free so that we would actually have freedom (see Gal 5:1). Are God's promises not relevant today? Is this freedom only metaphorical or merely freedom from serious sin?

We all have a sense of what it would look like for us to be spiritually free. We expect that we would be at peace, untroubled by fears, stress, or anxiety. If we were truly free, we would not get a sick feeling in our stomach when we thought about enduring a family Thanksgiving dinner; the mean words Aunt Maude spoke over us when we were six would no longer rankle. If we were free, we would have a solid core of joy inside, rather than a heavy weight that seems always present in our midsections.

The Church teaches us that receiving the Eucharist worthily gives us the grace to avoid continued sin. God not only truly forgives our sins through the sacrament of Reconciliation, but also gives us real help to stop sinning. What happens, though, when we cannot let go of what has already been dealt with through the sacraments and the cross of Christ? What happens when we go to confession, but the guilt and shame return even before we get into the car to go home? What do we do when the inner torment, the perverse thoughts, the tormenting accusations remain after we have followed the priest's instructions? Is it possible to not be consumed by repeated failures or even the expectation for evil and sin? What do we do with the sense of rejection and abandonment that is so strong that we cannot remember the truth of God's love for us? What if fear overcomes us? Can we live with fears like the fear of the future or the fear of the darkness of the past? Will we be able to get past a fear of poverty or a fear of committing the unforgivable sin? We remember that Jesus said, "Do not worry," and "I am with you," but the words seem absent of the power that they should have to pierce the darkness that surrounds us.

Many Catholics faced with these questions have turned to the realm of medicine and psychology for help. Indeed, we are blessed to have so much help available to us today. Yet scripture and the writings of the church fathers tell us that we find true freedom only in the Son of God. Jesus himself said, "If the Son makes you free, you will be free indeed" (Jn 8:36). When we are fully joined to Jesus Christ, then we are able to be fully human. St. Irenaeus proclaimed, "The glory of God is a human being fully alive." When we learn to live our life in the Son of God, then we can know that we are loved and treasured. You see, freedom means so much more than simply an absence of fear or stress. Freedom means that you *belong*.

Yes, *you*!

Freedom means that you know your true identity as a son of God; you know your place as a daughter of the loving Father. Freedom means that you can hear your true name spoken over you as you learn to believe that God loves you just the way he made you. Freedom means that you are able to fall in love with Jesus, and through him, fall in love with his Father.

The Church has provided teaching and the sacraments to help us encounter the Lord. In the normal life of a Catholic, we learn the importance of always returning to the grace of baptism in ongoing conversion. Through repentance, we turn back to God and rededicate ourselves as a disciple of Jesus. This is experienced in the sacrament of Reconciliation, where the priest declares absolution for our sins with all the authority that God has given his Church. Reconciliation properly prepares us to encounter Jesus in the Eucharist. The Church carries the message of freedom. Healing comes from God and is found in the Church as we bring our struggles to the Lord, receive forgiveness, forgive others, and take our stand against the lies that are incompatible with revealed truths.

And yet for so many, sin has become compulsive, and victory is not found through prayer or the sacraments. For so many, the hopelessness of repeated failure leads them to avoid Confession and to withdraw from the Eucharist. For so many, the excuses developed through distorted reasoning begin to sound like good justifications. "Why should I tell my sins to a priest when I can go directly to God?" they may say, or "Why does the Church have so many rules?" Some will even support sin by thinking, "If I am not harming anyone . . ."

But soon, the discomfort becomes a huge gulf, and they don't know how to return to God. What began as a struggle with sin has grown into enslavement in a swamp of darkness. This darkness is personal and has a name. The New Testament calls him Satan. We also know him as the devil.

I learned about the devil in my Catholic formation. In my grammar school, I remember a picture of a devil whispering into one ear of a child and an angel whispering into the other ear. It was clear that temptation to sin was from the devil. It was also clear that the devil was in charge of a terrible place called hell, and for sure I didn't want to go there! Only when I had a personal encounter with the love of God, however, did I become acutely aware of and understand the reality of the spiritual battle.

It is true that Christ has conquered all of our enemies:

> He disarmed the principalities and powers and made a public example of them, triumphing over them in him.
> — Col 2:15

Ultimately, Satan cannot hold any who belong to Christ. But, although the kingdom of darkness has been conquered, its prince and his demons are yet free to roam about and harm us. As St. Peter says:

> Be sober, be watchful. Your adversary the devil prowls around like a roaring lion, seeking some one to devour.
> — 1 Pet 5:8

This reality can lead many to fear. Just as love is the language of God, fear is the language of the devil. Fear — in particular, fear of the devil — distracts us from the complete trust that we are called to give to Jesus. The "father of lies" uses fear and deception to make us believe the lie that there is no help for us apart from ourselves. When the normal means of Catholic life and devotion have not dislodged the lie, then the people of God need to know that God has made provision for them.

God has given us both exorcism and deliverance as special provisions for spiritual warfare. Neither is well understood.

There is much fear about exorcism among the laity, just as there remains much skepticism about the work of the devil among the clergy. And the idea of deliverance prayer remains a completely new concept to both clergy and lay people.

EXORCISM AND DELIVERANCE

In the last thirty years, interest in exorcism has greatly increased, especially in Europe. I believe that God has been pouring out a grace on the Church that reveals the hidden work of the enemy at a time when there is an explosion of occult and New Age practices. Some of this increased interest is also fueled by the popular books of Gabriele Amorth and Fr. Jose Antonio Fortea, two internationally known exorcists.[3] Reports of Pope John Paul II praying for exorcism, as well as Mother Teresa receiving prayer of exorcism, furthered interest as these reports made international news. In 1999, the Church introduced the new Rite of Exorcism, marking the first change to the rite in almost 400 years. But, although it is becoming more common in the Church, many still fear exorcism — partly because of the way it is portrayed in movies, and partly because the direct confrontation with demons has caused some receiving prayer to manifest demonic forces that are frightening to them and to those who watch.

What exactly is exorcism? It is a liturgical rite of the Church, a sacramental provided for those cases where spiritual bondage has grown into possession. The person, no longer able to resist the enemy's control even with the prayer and support of others, needs a priest to step in and do battle against the enemy on his or her behalf. Exorcism is an unusual, extraordinary rite that should be used in only extreme cases of bondage.

Deliverance ministry, by contrast, should be a normal part of evangelization, even of the sacrament of Reconciliation. Yet it is not widely known outside the Charismatic Renewal in the Church.

So what, exactly, is deliverance? It is the effort — through prayer, counsel, or spiritual direction — to help someone take hold of the authority he has been given in Christ, defeat the enemy's lies, and break free of the oppression that afflicts him. It can be very attractive to think that only a holy priest can do battle against our demons, as in exorcism. But we should not be deceived. Every one of us needs to actively resist the tactics of the evil one and take responsibility for his life in Christ. An understanding of the principles of deliverance from the influence of evil spirits is important to every child of God. Even those who go through an exorcism have the responsibility to continue to walk in freedom and to know how to resist the devil's lies for the rest of their lives. We have this assurance from St. James:

> Submit yourselves therefore to God. Resist the devil and he will flee from you.
>
> — Jas 4:7

In my last book, *Unbound: a Practical Guide to Deliverance*,[4] I presented a model for receiving the freedom provided for us in Christ. Since writing the book, I have had the opportunity to help thousands of people take hold of the freedom that they have been given in Jesus. As my wife and I travel with this message, we get many questions from Catholics about exorcism, possession, demons, the authority of lay people, and how deliverance relates to the sacrament of Reconciliation. We find in those asking the questions a real desire to know the truth and to understand what the Church teaches. We also find a readiness to acknowledge the reality of evil spirits and the effect that they can have on the life of a Christian. People are aware that there is a power behind temptation. They understand that there really is a devil who wants us to sin and live under his influence, surrendering more and more of our freedom to him. Jesus tells us that anyone who sins is a slave to sin (Jn 8:34). He means more than that sin is an addiction. He means more than that sin ruptures our relationship with God. Jesus means that sin puts us under the power of the being that first sinned. We refer to that being in the Rite of baptism as "Satan, father of sin and prince of darkness."

One day, my wife told her hairdresser that we pray for people for freedom from spiritual bondage. The hairdresser interrupted Janet. "You mean demons! I have demons; I need that." A veteran of the Twelve-Step programs, she understood that her battle was greater than simply lack of will power or discipline issues. She was also fighting spiritual enemies.

More and more people are realizing the reality of spiritual forces. They realize that those forces can have influence in their lives if they have opened the door to their presence. Church leadership also recognizes this reality. In a general audience on November 15, 1972, Pope Paul VI began by saying:

> What are the Church's greatest needs at the present time? Don't be surprised at our answer and don't write it off as simplistic or even superstitious: one of the Church's greatest needs is to be defended against the evil we call the Devil.[5]

A moment later, he said:

> We come face to face with sin which is a perversion of human freedom and the profound cause of death because it involves detachment from God, the source of life. And then sin in its turn becomes the occasion and the effect of interference in us and our work by a dark, hostile agent, the Devil. Evil is not merely an absence of something but an active force, a living spiritual being that is perverted and that perverts others. It is a terrible reality, mysterious and frightening.

Cardinal Ratzinger, now Pope Benedict XVI, confirmed his predecessor's words when he was interviewed for the *Ratzinger Report:*

> Whatever the less discerning theologians may say, the devil, as far as Christian belief is concerned, is a puzzling but real, personal and not merely symbolical, presence.[6]

The Church understands what medical science does not: that behind the trauma passed down in families who experienced World War I, behind the personality disorders that affect so many young adults today, sits a malevolent being whose goal is to destroy our hope for a sound mind and our inheritance of a free will. Thankfully, the Church is beginning to teach her clergy the truths of spiritual warfare. The Regina Apostolorum Pontifical University in Rome made headlines when it began offering a course on "Exorcism and the Prayer of Deliverance." According to Carlo Climati, one of the teachers, the course was a response to the numerous requests that came from various parts of the world.[7]

Interest in the proper pastoral use of the sacred Rite of Exorcism also continues to gain momentum. In both 2007 and 2008, I had the privilege of attending a conference at Mundelein Seminary in Illinois, designed for priests and bishops to learn about exorcism and deliverance. Both exorcists with much expertise and sincere priests with no experience met to understand the new Rite of Exorcism and to learn how to better help those they serve. I discovered at that conference that many priests had very little teaching, if any, on the topics of deliverance and exorcism while in seminary.[8]

Many of our priests today were taught thirty or forty years ago to be suspicious of the existence of the devil and of the possibility that evil spirits could affect people's lives. Psychology became a new religion for some, and this "new religion" had its effect on many seminaries at the time, for good and for bad. What is taught in the seminaries in one generation is worked out in the parishes in the next.

I also learned that many exorcists had little understanding of deliverance ministry, and many in deliverance ministry have a great deal to learn about the Church's approach to exorcism. I am encouraged that a pontifical university is teaching on "Exorcism and the Prayer of Deliverance," for I believe the relationship between the two approaches needs to be studied so that each will complement the other as God intends.

A MATTER OF DEGREE

In the spiritual realm, we find a wide range of demonic activity. On one end of the spectrum is temptation; on the other end is possession by a demon. Temptation leads to sin; sin, if not healed, may lead to compulsion and further loss of freedom. Sin and all the works of the devil are designed to bring us progressively into deeper bondage. Like cancer, sin spreads its negative effects to other parts of one's life if left untreated. The deeper bondage a person experiences, the greater the need for help that goes beyond the regular practice of the Faith.

Deliverance is a normal means God has given us to resist the devil, a ministry that can rescue the believer at almost any stage of rebellion. Deliverance ministry could be considered any authentically Christian means by which people help others overcome the devil's influence in their lives, and it should take place in the ordinary life of a Catholic.

In the sacrament of Reconciliation, the penitent experiences deliverance and slips out from the enemy's grip as he reclaims his baptismal grace by confessing his sins and receiving absolution. But deliverance may also take place through prayers of intercession. When Jesus taught his disciples to pray, he was teaching us as well to pray, "Deliver us from the evil one" (Mt 6:13, NAB). Deliverance may also take place as part of spiritual direction or a retreat, or may come as the truth is proclaimed. As you can see, the normality of deliverance means that every

Catholic can serve as a minister to another as we evangelize our friends, helping them offer a more complete "yes," like Mary's *fiat*, to Jesus Christ.

At the extreme outer edge of the spectrum of demonic activity lies demonic possession, for which the Church's Rite of Exorcism may be the only solution. When I refer to exorcism here, I'm not referring to the simple exorcism of baptism or of the catechumenate. In contrast with something performed yearly, like the St. Blaise's blessing of throats or the renewal of baptismal vows, true exorcism is and should be very rare. It is a very special provision that has been made for people who, over time, have submerged and lost their true identity to a demonic power. In exorcism, the afflicted one steps aside as the priest confronts the demonic spirits, seeking to drive them out through the use of the sacred liturgical ritual of the Church. This liturgical rite is only to be used for those who have been determined by the Church to be possessed.

Unfortunately, there is a great deal of confusion over what constitutes possession, whether an exorcism is warranted, what deliverance ministry really is, and who in the Church has the right to minister deliverance, anyway. As long ago as 1983, Léon Cardinal Suenens published a book entitled *Renouveau et Puissances des Ténèbres* (*Renewal and the Powers of Darkness*). In it, he pointed to the present-day confusion that results from a failure to address the need for deliverance of those who are not possessed:

> Cases of genuine possession, which only the bishop or his delegate may deal with, are rare. But everything that falls short of possession in the strict sense remains a blurred, ill-defined area where confusion and ambiguity prevail.[9]

I believe that the gift that God gives the church in the Rite of Exorcism will not be seen it its proper perspective unless there is a wider understanding of deliverance ministry. By the same token, deliverance ministry will not be understood until it is seen in the context of evangelization, the proclamation of the Kingdom of God. Evangelization is incomplete, of course, unless it brings us into the reality of our baptism through which we were "delivered from the dominion of darkness and transferred to the kingdom of his beloved Son" (Col 1:13).

The purpose of this book is to shed light on the "blurred, ill-defined" distinctions between exorcism and deliverance that are confusing and ambiguous and to show how they fit into the life of the Catholic parish. Above all, my purpose is to show how the Lord's freedom can be gained and held through deliverance, so that the need for exorcism will rarely arise.

By examining exorcism and deliverance as two paths to spiritual freedom, I am not minimizing the gift of the sacrament of Reconciliation, the primary means God has given Catholics to break with the bondage of sin and receive spiritual freedom. But by focusing on exorcism and deliverance, I hope to help overcome some of the confusion that masks the gift God has provided. In the final chapters, I will reflect on how the sacraments, exorcism, and deliverance ministry are interwoven as the Church continues the ministry of Jesus, who came to "destroy the works of the devil" (1 Jn 3:8) and "to set at liberty those who are oppressed" (Lk 4:18).

CHAPTER 2

Do I Need an Exorcism?

The spiritual battle against the enslaving forces, the exorcism over a world blinded by demons, is an inseparable part of the spiritual way of Jesus and his disciples.

— Manfred Hauke

To examine exorcism and deliverance simply from a viewpoint of theory or theology is to miss the point. Exorcism and deliverance are ministries of compassion to real people with real struggles. One who comes for exorcism or deliverance is not unlike you or me. In fact, you might even identify with Rebecca. (Note: Some names have been altered for the sake of privacy.)

Rebecca grew up in a close-knit family. Her parents were members of the Charismatic Renewal, and were deeply committed to their Catholic faith. Church, sacraments, family prayer, and prayer with guests were simply part of her youth. However, as a teen, she felt embarrassed about being religious and began to be drawn into the lives of her high-school friends rather than family. She became rebellious against the Lord and the life that her parents offered to her. At age twenty-five, she married a man with whom she had partied. As they went through the struggles of the first year of marriage, she and her husband came back to the Lord and the Church.

During the early years of marriage, they experienced a lot of healing, and as their conversion deepened, Rebecca would move from crisis to surrender. In one of these moments of awareness of her deep need, she asked her family to pray over her. As they prayed, her father suggested that she renounce the spirit of the Antichrist. (Whether this was revelation from heaven or simply his idea, I don't know.) When he mentioned the name of the Antichrist, she put her head in her hands and began to scream. She later described it as experiencing a fear that was far beyond anything she could imagine. It seemed to her not her own fear, but the devil's fear, coming from the pit of hell.

Two days later, she came to my wife, Janet, for ministry. As she began to tell her story of what happened, fear gripped her again, and she found her face turning away from Janet, unable to look into her eyes. Does she need exorcism? Should Janet refer her to the diocese? We will come back to these questions at the end of the chapter, after we have clarified some of the confusions about exorcism and deliverance.

Across the world, in Africa, priests ask similar questions about their parishioners. Leaders there have come to expect manifestations of evil such as grinding of teeth, falling to the floor in a tormented state, rolling back of the eyes, and even blacking out. Janet and I were in Kenya five years ago, teaching parish leaders how to approach deliverance ministry in a way that would provoke very little, if any, manifestations. The leaders were so relieved when they saw that the Lord set people free without a big disturbance.

"Oh, you mean we don't have to shout anymore?" they asked us — a declaration of liberation as much as a question. "But this doesn't work in all cases, does it?"

"Why do you ask?" I replied.

"Recently, we were asked by the parish priest of a border town to do a Life in the Spirit seminar. When we mentioned the name of Jesus, about eighty people fell on the ground manifesting demonically."

After this happened, the leaders had left that outreach very frustrated and discouraged. Later, they had discovered that in that town, straddling Tanzania and Kenya, everyone had been dedicated to the devil as a child. It was no wonder that so many reacted to the name of Jesus!

Did all these people need exorcisms, then? If they all did, where could the leaders find enough priests to help all of them? Or did they need deliverance?

Again, let's return to these questions after a discussion that explains the difference between exorcism and deliverance.

UNDERSTANDING THE PLACE OF EXORCISM AND DELIVERANCE

There is an undeniable need for understanding and teaching about exorcism and deliverance. One priest told me that in his country, although the exorcists get together, they can never agree on anything. In another country, my book *Unbound* was given to a number of exorcists to evaluate for publication. Some loved it; others thought I didn't know what I was talking about! In Rwanda, a highly respected bishop has adopted the five keys of the Unbound Model and put them in a booklet on healing, to be distributed throughout the country. In yet another country, a priest friend of mine was asked to participate with the official exorcist and left distressed by what he saw. He witnessed people, coming regularly for exorcism, who had to be tied down while the demons were tormented by the prayers. Some individuals would come week after week, for up to twelve months, before they were free. Many, many others *never* got free. Hundreds of people in many countries inquire about exorcism each month, but multitudes more never ask for help because of confusion about exorcism and deliverance.

Confusion about exorcism exists, in part, because the word *possession* is often used interchangeably with words like *oppression* or *obsession* that describe lesser degrees of influence. Some think that anyone who has been set free of the influences of an evil spirit was possessed. Often, one who says he had an "exorcism" means simply that he has been set free, while others really do mean that they had the Rite of Exorcism said over them.

Movies and books on exorcism and possession have had added to popular confusion. They draw attention to the devil and give him a chance to demonstrate his agenda. In some books, the focus is so much on the devil and the action of the priest that the humanity of the afflicted person appears to be ignored.

Fr. Francis Martin, a highly regarded Scripture scholar, has appealed openly for more schools of training in exorcism and deliverance. Many people, even holy people, have an irrational fear of the devil because of the mystery that surrounds possession and exorcism, and the need is great.

Exorcism as a Pastoral Issue

The Church has long cared for those whom the devil has bound and tormented through the liturgical Rite of Exorcism. This rite developed in the Church through the centuries to help those possessed by the devil. The solemn Rite of Exorcism, a sacramental of the Church, can only be used by a priest with the bishop's permission, so it can be confusing when people use the word *exorcism* to describe other forms of deliverance. To avoid this confusion, let me clarify how I am using certain terms.

Exorcism, as I have said, is the liturgical rite of the Catholic Church used to drive out evil spirits. The *Catechism* (1673) defines exorcism as a public and authoritative command "in the name of Jesus Christ that a person or object be protected against the power of the Evil One and withdrawn from his dominion."

The word "public" in this context is often misunderstood. As Fr. Jeffrey Grob writes in his doctoral thesis:

> An exorcism is considered "public" when an authorized person using an approved rite does it in the name of the Church. A "private" exorcism is not bound by the same constraints and may be celebrated by any of the faithful.[10]

Indeed, it was common for Christians in the early years of the Church to drive out spirits as part of the work of evangelization. St. Irenaeus (second century AD) indicated that the driving out of demons was part of normal evangelization that led people to believe in Christ and join the Church:

> Wherefore, also, those who are in truth his disciples, receiving grace from him, do in his name perform [miracles], so as to promote the welfare of other men, according to the gift which each one has received from him. For some do certainly and truly drive out devils, so that those who have thus been cleansed fromevil spirits frequently both believe [in Christ], and join themselves to the Church.[11]

Only after several hundred years did the Church begin to establish boundaries around exorcism. She did this to care for both those who were truly possessed and for all who suffered under lesser degrees of demonic influence. In any case, exorcism came to be associated with a ritual that most often included a confrontation with demons, the manifesting of demons, the seeking of demons' names, and finally, the driving out of demons. Exorcism moves beyond the focus on the individual to the priest's battle with the demon on his behalf.

Deliverance, though a ministry of the universal Church, is not circumscribed by an official rite. It appears in two forms: confrontational and non-confrontational. Any deliverance ministry that confronts demons on behalf of the victim, seeking information from the demons, is a confrontational or an "exorcism" style of deliverance. The ministry might or might not use any ritual or formula other than the command to the demon to leave in the name of Jesus. But what it does have in common with exorcism is provoking and driving the demon out on behalf of the person to whom they minister.

In contrast, my primary experience is with the non-confrontational style of deliverance, which I will refer to as the

"Unbound Model." In this model, the focus always remains on the person and not the demon. The one ministering draws the information needed from the individual in cooperation with the Holy Spirit's revelation. Once the entryway for an evil spirit's presence is uncovered, repentance, forgiveness, and renunciation break the power of its influence. Then speaking a command for spirits to depart confirms the victory or opens the door for deeper revelation of darkness. Prayer to receive the Father's blessing completes the process. The Unbound Model calls these five elements of deliverance prayer the "Five Keys."

Exorcism is the only framework that many Catholics outside of charismatic circles have to address the needs of those in bondage to, or under oppression by, evil spirits. The Church's prescribed remedy for possession by an evil spirit is exorcism. But many do not understand lesser degrees of demonic influence such as oppression or obsession. Nor does the Church prescribe a specific remedy for these conditions. This limited perspective can lead to tragic results.

Let me share an example that is a composite of several people's stories. Let's assume that John experiences the presence of evil or spiritual bondage that he believes is connected to the prince of darkness. His anger, out of control at times, is more aptly described as rage. He hates himself for the damage he is doing to his wife and children. He goes to a priest and asks for help. He may be dismissed with a few brief words of advice, or sent for counseling — perhaps to someone who doesn't even believe in the devil. Still seeking help, he talks to another priest, one more open to the possibility that the problem has a demonic source, who refers John to someone with more experience. Along the way, the message John receives is that he cannot have an exorcism unless he is possessed. Yet exorcism appears to be his only hope. Realizing that he will have to prove the spiritual nature of his problem to a psychiatrist, he may then begin to build a case in his mind as to why he is possessed. He labels himself and attempts to convince others so that he can receive an exorcism. John sees an exorcism as the only help beyond confession, the sacraments, prayer, and sacrifice, which he has already tried.

The result is that John looks at the power of darkness within and identifies with it. He may delve into it, unwittingly going deeper down the path of bondage by embracing the label of being a person possessed by the devil and in need of an exorcism. Many people like John — in some cases having had "exorcisms" without finding relief — now see themselves as possessed and helpless unless they can find a holier priest or a more anointed person to help them.

This unenlightened process can follow other paths as well. Mary may go for a confrontational style of deliverance prayer and find herself manifesting demonic presences. As the demons are confronted, it may seem like the more she allows the evil spirits to manifest in and through her body, the closer she is to getting free. Her relief is great.

"Now somebody believes me and can help me," she may think. "Finally, what has been buried inside is coming to the surface."

But if the issue is not resolved that day, she, too, might begin to see herself as "possessed' at some level and helpless, needing more of an exorcist type of deliverance. The results may be even more tragic if John or Mary has a psychological or emotional disorder, in addition to the spiritual bondage, that is not being addressed. Adding the self-diagnostic word "possessed" may contribute to John's fragile sense of identity or Mary's emotional instability.

The Loss of Identity

The devil's work has always been to steal our identity as children of God and to take from us our life's purpose. Unfortunately, we can play into his hand by taking on the identity of a "possessed" person with little ability to resist the devil. But in truth, our core identity is that we are children of God — and not just little children, but sons and daughters with dignity and responsibility. Genesis tells us that God entrusted us with responsibility for His creation:

> And God blessed them, and God said to them, "Be fruitful and multiply and fill the earth and subdue it; and have dominion over the fish of the sea and over the birds of the air and over every living thing that moves upon the earth."
>
> — Gen 1:28

God wants us to rule. Authority is something that has been restored to us through life in Christ. But in the examples above, John and Mary forsook their true identities in the process of seeking help. As they embraced the idea that they were possessed, each actually lost sight of his identity as a child of God and gave up the authority he holds as a son (or daughter) of God.

CAN A BELIEVER BE COMPLETELY POSSESSED?

Possession is the word commonly used in the Church to identify those who qualify for the Rite of Exorcism. Demonic possession means a door has been opened to a fallen angel — a demonic force — and that a person's will has been submerged and he is no longer able to resist the devil's lies and torturous activities. Further, the condition of possession is one in which there are signs that an evil spirit has gained access, not simply to aspects of thinking and will but also to a person's actual body. In such a case, the demon "at specific moments can speak and move through [the body] without the person being able to prevent this."[12] However, even though in the Rite of Exorcism the Church lists certain signs of demonic possession as indicators that someone may be considered possessed, these indicators should not be considered apart from an evaluation of the whole person and his life of faith.[13]

The wisdom the Church follows is analogous to a medical approach: just as a doctor observes groups of symptoms and performs tests to attempt to determine a definitive cause of disease, so the official exorcist will consider all the signs and evidence of possession in the context of the Catholic's life of faith. Just as a doctor may begin to treat symptoms to relieve distress prior to determining the definitive cause, so the Church directs the exorcist to address particular signs of spiritual distress through various means of grace available to Catholics. These include the sacraments, prayer and fasting, evangelization, catechesis, spiritual direction, or deliverance ministry. Beginning to relieve symptoms of disease quickly may, in fact, protect the patient from the aggressive response of surgery. In like manner, beginning to address the typical outward signs of evil influences with available graces may protect the penitent from the aggressive treatment of exorcism.

It is also helpful to distinguish a lesser form of possession from "complete possession," where the individual has so completely surrendered his will to a demon that he no longer desires anything other than evil. Rather than struggling against the evil within, he revels in it. We can all think of examples from history, or the news, of that kind of embrace with darkness. A man or woman who initiates horrendous wickedness and shows no remorse is but one example of one who may have allowed a spirit to clothe himself in his body and take over his personality. A union has been achieved; he is completely possessed.

A troubled Christian may wonder, "Can I be occupied and taken over by an evil spirit?" The short answer is "No." The thought that demons fly around and can land on anyone they choose is a myth. If someone has had a conversion, embracing the truth revealed in baptism, she cannot be *completely* possessed unless she purposely forsakes that gift. In the face of demonic harassment or internal battle, the Christian can take her stand based upon the truth of the Gospel. By grace, she has become a temple of the Holy Spirit. God dwells within, and in a very real sense, her life is no longer her own; she now belongs to God. In

Romans 8, we read that nothing can separate us from the love of God. Nothing means *nothing*, and that *includes* all the powers of hell. In the face of attack, there is a place within her where she can call upon the Lord and in His name proclaim: "He who is in you (me) is greater than he who is in the world" (1 Jn 4:4).

However, if someone is baptized but not fully evangelized, he may — through deception, abuse, neglect, or a combination of reasons — seek some sort of connection in the spirit realm. The person may not be aware of the evil or just not be concerned about the source. Perhaps because of his pain, he may recklessly go after companionship, comfort, answers, or purpose. He may be seeking a "spiritual guide," "spiritual power," or some other entity that disguises evil as an angel of light. The deeper he enters into the relationship with the spirit, the further he moves toward the possibility of possession. A person who has been introduced to demons as a child through abuse, occult practice, or even by being dedicated to the devil by his parents, may continue, through ignorance, down the road toward possession. Though others have opened the doorway to evil, he allows the enemy to act by persisting in going through that door.

So what does the Church mean when it uses the term *possession*? It means that the person is severely demonized and on a path toward complete possession. Sometimes, a man or woman who began to follow the Lord will turn away. He or she may actively reject the Lord and prefer deception. Most people who qualify for an exorcism seem to be moving uncontrollably in the direction of complete possession, but they are tormented by what is going on. They are not yet completely possessed because they are asking for help, either verbally or nonverbally — acting out in a way that's clearly a cry for help. They are like the demon-possessed man among the tombs who came to Jesus. If he had been completely possessed, he would not have come to Jesus.

The Church uses the word *possession* only in cases where there is need for a solemn exorcism. This means that in these extreme cases, the Church is there to snatch people from the enemy's attempt to hold them in slavery. In an exorcism, the priest confronts the devil in the name of Jesus and the Church, on behalf of the person who is "possessed." Although the victim's cooperation is essential, he is on the sidelines during the battle and afterward may have no memory, or very little memory, of what transpired. His lack of memory is no doubt grace for him, for the reality of possession — and even the thought of it — is troubling.

As Christians, we must be prepared to come alongside the afflicted individual and help him believe in who he truly is in Christ. As we do this, we must use great care in the terms we use. Although the term "possession" does need to be used in the study and discussion of exorcism and demonology, and though it must also be used as part of the investigative procedure related to a request for exorcism, helping someone understand what it means to be possessed and to qualify for an exorcism must be done with love. A doctor will use care in talking to a patient. He doesn't just come out and say, "I think you have cancer," but instead says, "Let's do some more tests." Then he will call the patient into the office so that he may explain the diagnosis carefully in its broader context.

Can a Believer Be Controlled by Evil Spirits?

Can evil spirits control a believer? Yes and no. Church history records that evil spirits have afflicted some saints.[14] The devil uses many schemes against us. Even the fear of possession can entrap us and draw us into further bondage. When a believer experiences demonic harassment, the devil might feed him thoughts such as "The devil is in control," or "I have committed the unforgivable sin; I am lost," or "God cannot save me," or "I must be possessed." When one dwells on the possibility of being possessed, he opens the door to these lies, and thus to the downward spiral of increased helplessness and surrender. If the

Christian thinks he is under the enemy's control, the enemy has already gained a significant foothold.

As I wrote in *Unbound*, it appears that it would be better to translate the Greek word "possessed" as "demonized." The Greek word means "to have a demon" or to "act under the control of a demon." But *acting* under the control of a demon does not necessarily mean the person is possessed. We can choose to submit to acting under the control of a demon or not. Anyone undergoing spiritual or physical affliction in life may turn that suffering into a path of holiness. That is what some afflicted saints were able to do. But it is a mistake to "make friends" with a demonic affliction, thinking it is from God. Yes, God allows evils for his mysterious purposes, but he calls us to resist and take our stand against all of the schemes of the devil (Jas 4:7; Eph 6:11). We need to understand that God is pleased to reveal his Son to us, in us and through us (cf. Gal 1:16), not through demonic forces.

Ministering with Compassion

The discussion of exorcism and deliverance raises pastoral questions to be addressed as well. One psychiatrist concurred with me that letting a victim manifest demonically week after week, as she goes through repeated exorcisms, could be like the experience of "cutting" or purging. Another internationally known Catholic psychologist expressed concern about ongoing exorcism with those who get so much attention, love, prayer and touch, and yet remain bound. She theorizes that there may be a human reason why the person doesn't find freedom: the presence of a demonic force may have been his only doorway to such love and attention.[15]

This confusion isn't surprising — the devil is the master of disorder and confusion. The devil always wants to present himself as stronger, more powerful, and more in control than he really is. We have to be very careful not to treat someone as possessed if he is not. We could end up playing the devil's game.

It's been said that the devil's greatest deception is getting us to believe that he doesn't exist. This even seems to be his preference, to disguise his activity in order to keep the Church from addressing the real issue. But if he is exposed, then he wants to be the center of attention, drawing our thoughts away from God, provoking fear to replace the love that comes from Him. Freedom is found in focusing on Jesus, our savior and deliverer, who has absolute authority over the enemy and who sets us free to know the love of the Father.

HELP IN THE CHURCH

There are a growing number of dedicated and holy priests heroically committed to the work of exorcism. If not for their dedication, many who have been helped would have continued to struggle in bondage to evil. At the conference on healing, deliverance, and exorcism that I attended at Mundelein Seminary, I witnessed a deep hunger among priests to assist those afflicted by evil spirits. Many of them have poured themselves out sacrificially to bring liberation to those who are bound or possessed. The Church really is the place of healing for those in bondage.

TWO STORIES OF DELIVERANCE

Now let us return to Rebecca and our friends in Kenya.

You will recall that Rebecca could not look at Janet because of the fear that gripped her from within. First, Janet gently encouraged Rebecca to look at her and reminded her that in Jesus Christ, she had the ability to do it. Janet then spoke directly, and with authority: "In the name of Jesus, look at me." Rebecca described it later this way:

> Once my eyes met Janet's, I melted. It was as if I was looking into God the Father's eyes, eyes of love for me. I was safe. Janet asked me some questions and then, as I had done on another occasion, I rededicated myself to

the Lord. I pronounced forgiveness to those who hurt me and I renounced several things. Then Janet said, "Now renounce the lie that Jesus is not the Truth." As soon as I renounced it, the fear that gripped me broke. When Janet commanded the spirit to leave, I felt deeper freedom. Then I received her prayers of blessing. Every morning for the next week, the first thought that came to mind as I opened my eyes was, "Jesus is the Truth."

Freedom comes from knowing Jesus is the Truth. The lie that gripped Rebecca's heart had taken hold of her when she was a teenager. Now, that lie was incompatible with her life as she sought to be a disciple of the Lord — but despite her past repentance and prayers, the lie held on from within because of her past agreement with it. This lie wasn't just a foolish thought. It was an area of spiritual bondage. The conflict within led her to ask for prayer again. When her family prayed for her, they named the demon that was the source of the lie; when it was named, it showed up to do its best to intimidate and distract Rebecca from recognizing the lie.

A disconnect between past experiences and current struggles can leave a believer thinking that the devil can come and possess her in the future any time she doesn't pray all of her prayers or thinks she has failed in the Christian life. She may lose her sense of personal authority over her own spiritual well being, forgetting that God equipped each of us to fight our own spiritual enemies as part of the normal Christian life. She may believe someone else needs to battle for her. Uncovering the connection between the past and the present trouble is part of our task as we minister to her. This is a major reason why our focus must always be on the person, rather than on a demon.

Now, back to the situation in Kenya, where my friends were confronting what seemed to be a need for mass exorcisms. I told them, however, that I thought the non-confrontational style of the Unbound Model could work in that town where so many had been dedicated to the devil. It would require that they approach deliverance differently.

They decided that they would take Fr. Peter, their pastor and an Irish missionary, with them. He began the service by telling the folks that he did not want them to manifest — that is, to show physical reactions such as shouts, twisting of the face, blacking out, and so on. Immediately, two people fell out and began to manifest demonically on the floor. Fr. Peter went over to them and said, "I bind these spirits in the name of Jesus and command you to be still." Those two people lay motionless for the next twelve hours. After that, I think the people were more afraid of Fr. Peter than the devil!

(Though I don't normally recommend this methodology, it is an example of how God can use us in unique ways.)

Next, Fr. Peter carried the Blessed Sacrament around the room; anyone who could not look up was invited into the next room for an interview, where they were led through the five keys that are the core of the Unbound Model. Stephen T., one of the leaders on that mission trip, described the meetings in this way:

> Our mission trip was a tough one, but God was glorified. All those who opened themselves up to the Lord's deliverance were set free. Leah and I arrived there on the evening of deliverance ministry; Fr. Peter had already given the teaching in the conventional method. We entered into the ministry and applied the new model of Unbound ministry to those that had demonic manifestation. There were over one hundred people who could not lift their heads to look at the Blessed Sacrament. We witnessed success in all cases except for a few who were bound in witchcraft and were not ready to renounce. Some of those were minors dedicated by their parents to the evil kingdom who were still under the authority of their parents.

The crowd comprised about two hundred and fifty people who saw the hand of God at work by the Holy Spirit. Their lives were changed from misery and desperation into a joyous crowd full of hope, ready to face the future in the power of the Holy Spirit.

The Kenyan believers did not need an exorcism; they needed someone to help them take up the authority given to them in faith and baptism. They needed to expose the entryways in their lives, to name them, and to renounce them.

Does this mean they are totally free? Perhaps not, but it does mean they have tools to face the next area of conflict that will arise as they, like Rebecca, seek to live as disciples of Jesus. Living as a disciple will lead to an inner conflict with any hidden sin, unforgiveness, deception, or false understanding of God's love. We all need the tools to fight for our freedom. It was an African who actually said to me, "You have not given us a fish; you are teaching us how to fish."

Do you need an exorcism? Probably not. But you may need deliverance from the influence of evil spirits, from obsession or oppression. Any Catholic who submits to the lordship of Christ can learn to minister this deliverance to others, helping them to take up the necessary personal responsibility for the normal Christian life of freedom.

The Church provides exorcism for the extreme cases. The need for exorcism arises when someone is unable, even with the help of others, to freely pursue her freedom. It is only in one's inability to break free, using all the means of grace that God has provided, that the need for exorcism is clear. Exorcism is outside the mainstream of Church life, but deliverance is not.

As we pursue the Lord, we can expect the truth of the Gospel to continually expose the lies of the enemy, making it possible for us to enter more completely into the freedom Christ has for us. This is our inheritance: "For freedom Christ has set us free" (Gal 5:1).

CHAPTER 3

Do I Need Deliverance?

Since therefore the children share in flesh and blood, he himself likewise partook of the same nature, that through death he might destroy him who has the power of death, that is, the devil, and deliver all those who through fear of death were subject to lifelong bondage.

— Heb 2:14-15

"Hello, this is Fr. Francis from the Office of Canonical Services. How can I help you?"

"Father, I called because I do not know who else to call. I think I need an exorcism." The voice on the line was hesitant. "My parish priest doesn't think so, but so many strange things have happened to me in my life, I am now convinced it is because of the devil."

"Why do you think you may need an exorcism?" Fr. Francis asked.

"I was reading a book by Fr. Gabriele Armoth, *An Exorcist Tells His Story,* and some of the stories sounded like things I have experienced. It was the first time things seemed to make sense to me — I think I've been cursed."

Fortunately, there are priests like Fr. Francis. He is the key contact in a large diocese in the United States for people who are wondering about exorcism. Having written a book on deliverance, I, too, get many similar requests for help. Each story is different. The person may say, "I have these compulsive thoughts about killing myself," or "Blasphemous thoughts go through my mind at the consecration during Mass." Another might say, "When I close my eyes at night, I see evil faces," or "Sometimes I wake up from sleep and feel a presence in my room." Yet another might confess, "I know things about people I should not know," or "I think someone has put a curse on me, I hear voices." In some way, each person expresses that he is being tormented. Some of the calls come from those whose loved ones have been dabbling in the occult or listening to music about the devil, all with disastrous effects on their lives and relationships.

Fr. Francis may receive as many as 400 calls in a year. Some callers are experiencing a sense of the presence of evil or seeing things move in their house — but more often, they're just asking for help with inner torment that has not been relieved though confession, prayer, and Eucharist. Some calls come from people who have been away from the Church, who don't understand how living a life of devotion to God is fundamental to living in freedom. Many people calling for exorcism don't realize that the basis for freedom is our relationship with Christ, and that each of us has an essential part to play in taking hold of our own freedom. An exorcist cannot do battle on our behalf without our cooperation, for each of us is responsible for our own response to the lies of the enemy, both in the past and in the present.

Fr. Francis listens with compassion and understanding to every call, even though he knows from experience that only two or three people a year will qualify for an exorcism. He does know the devil is real — a great relief to many callers. He also knows that very rarely is an exorcism the answer to someone's true need, so he will try to help the caller get the appropriate care. Perhaps that care is advice from a spiritual director or guidance from a parish priest, a medical doctor, or a mental health professional. Sometimes, however, an experienced priest or layperson who prays for deliverance is the answer.

Calling a priest like Fr. Francis is a great blessing to someone in trouble. Compassion, understanding, and a worldview that does not exclude or minimize the possibility of the devil's influence in one's life is liberating in itself. Fr. Francis provides a great service to those who are tormented. Anguish and fear are always compounded when there is no one to listen or understand.

Unfortunately, not every parishioner in trouble reaches a Fr. Francis. Some priests may quickly, even abruptly, refer a caller to a mental health professional while discounting or simply minimizing her spiritual concerns. Such a response will contribute to her embarrassment. She may think something is wrong with her and that nobody understands. Other priests may even go beyond discounting the possibility of the devil's influence and actually scorn the caller, placing her in a position of being forced to either deny or reinterpret her experience in order to fit an acceptable framework. One parishioner brought a desperate young man looking for an exorcism to her priest — only to have him respond, "Oh, the Church doesn't do that anymore." If this happens, a person will receive no help in understanding the ways the devil can influence us through temptations and deception.

Many priests haven't received any practical training in this area in the seminary. They may have been affected in the '60s and '70s by an attitude that a "superior" understanding of psychology had replaced the traditional view of the devil as a cause of our turmoil. Priests could now send people in need to the professionals, relieving themselves of the responsibility. Although myriad benefits have come from the study of the human person and our emotional and psychological development, psychology will never replace the uniquely spiritual help that only the Church can give. A psychological, behavioral, or cognitive approach can never completely heal problems that include a spiritual component.

Not only have many priests not had good theology about the devil, but also, very few have learned anything about deliverance apart from the Rite of Exorcism and the normal Catholic life of faith. Most are aware that a certain degree of freedom flows supernaturally from receiving the sacraments regularly and worthily. However, if a person does not get the help he needs through these means, little else is available. If only two out of the 400 who call Fr. Francis need an exorcism, I wonder about all the others. How many might benefit from deliverance ministry along with the other recommendations of prayer, sacraments, spiritual counseling or direction, and therapeutic help?

What Is Deliverance Ministry?

Deliverance ministry is a participation in the ministry of Jesus, who came to set the captives free, deliver us from the power of sin, and destroy the works of the devil. It is the ministry of the whole Church.

Often, people understand deliverance ministry specifically as a form of minor exorcism, because it is directed at driving out evil spirits. But the meaning of the word *deliverance* is much richer and deeper than the ministry of casting out evil spirits or even the remnants of their influence. To understand deliverance ministry, we need to first see deliverance ministry in its broader context.

"Deliverance" Is a Good Word

Deliverance happened to you when you were baptized, and when you first accepted the Faith of your parents and godparents as your own. You were transferred from the dominion of darkness to the kingdom of God's Son, as Paul tells us in Colossians 1:13. Deliverance involves taking hold of the full freedom that God has given you in His kingdom. Let me share one simple example of deliverance that I received from a participant at one of our conferences.

> I have struggled with anger and criticism toward my husband that I have been unable to control for years. I understood the root cause, but was still unable to get a handle on it. At the conference, I repented, and renounced everything having to do with that subject

that I could. I forgave everyone I could think of, as well. I was not sure if anything significant had happened.

During the talk about staying free on the last day, the speaker told her own story, which was similar to mine. She mentioned having to repent of withdrawing her heart from her own father and from God. I was surprised, but the thought stayed with me for the rest of the day.

On the drive home, I thought through what the speaker had said, and I began to feel I had to say it as well. I repented very loudly for withdrawing my heart from my father, from God, and from my husband. I broke down and started to sob for several minutes. I renounced, and took command and felt like a weight had been lifted off my shoulders.

It wasn't long before my first test. The very next morning, my husband and I began to argue. Normally, I would shout back and get defensive. Instead, for the first time in my marriage, I actually cried! I told my husband that he really hurt me when he yelled at me. I could not believe it was me! For the first time in so long, I felt like my heart was opening to him.

God is so good and so faithful. I am trying hard to stay free and use the five steps when I start falling into old patterns. Sometimes I succeed and sometimes I don't, but I'm still in the fight, with God's help.

The concept of deliverance ministry has very negative connotations for many people. Sometimes, I am introduced by someone who says, "Well, Neal Lozano has this great healing ministry." He will go on about healing and then say, in a hushed tone, "He also does deliverance." The word provokes a distinct lack of enthusiasm in many, and, unfortunately, often brings up images of the devil and people in anguish manifesting the presence of evil spirits. It raises fears of humiliation and embarrassment or memories of past abuse. Many well-documented abuses in deliverance have provided a valid basis for such a response — but I want to say that "deliverance" is a *good* word.

Deliverance is one of the great themes of Scripture. Israel was delivered out of bondage to Pharaoh and brought into the Promised Land. After seventy years of captivity in Babylon, the Jews were delivered and brought to Jerusalem. They celebrate their deliverance every year at the most significant feast, the feast of Passover. At Passover, they remember and ask the question: "Why is this night unlike any other night?" And they tell the story of how God, by His mighty power, led them out of bondage in Egypt and into the Promised Land. They were slaves who were redeemed. *Their identity as slaves was overshadowed by their identity as God's chosen people.* This is the story that that Joseph and Mary told Jesus when he was growing up. Deliverance is primarily his story. In Jesus, the fulfillment of the promise of deliverance is completed, and he opens the door to our own deliverance.

Now deliverance is our story, too. We read about it in Colossians 1:13-14:

> For he has delivered us from the dominion of darkness and brought us into the kingdom of the Son he loves, in whom we have redemption, the forgiveness of sins.

We have been delivered in Christ. Deliverance *is* a good word!

DELIVERANCE FROM DARKNESS TO LIGHT

In the world of the Old Testament, before Jesus came and manifested the Kingdom of God, Scripture says that "darkness [would] cover the whole earth" (Is 60:2). But the darkness was not fully perceived because the tremendous contrast between light and darkness was dulled. Only when Jesus came as the Light was darkness revealed for what it was. In the New Testament, the meaning and significance of the darkness becomes clear. 1 John 5:19 tells us, "The whole world is in the power of the evil one."

When Jesus commissioned Paul to proclaim the Gospel to the Gentiles, he said, "I send you to open their eyes, that they may turn from darkness to light and from the power of Satan to God" (Acts 26:17b-18). Jesus was not speaking vaguely about spiritual realities or metaphorically about two kingdoms. He sent Paul to deliver people, take them out from under Satan's authority, and place them under His lordship.

Unfortunately, many people hear the word deliverance and think that it concerns only the devil or exorcism. But deliverance also describes the salvation won for us in Christ and the power to regularly live the abundant life that Jesus promised. Deliverance is a good word; through it, relationships with God and others are restored so that we can give and receive love without any obstacles. Deliverance enables us to walk in our true identity as sons and daughters of God, daily able to experience the freedom of not having our past poison our healthy present and future. Yes, deliverance is a very good word indeed!

DELIVERANCE IN THE SACRAMENT OF BAPTISM

Our greatest deliverance has already taken place through baptismal faith. If we know Jesus, we know freedom. When a Catholic is experiencing spiritual torment, he must be reminded of the truth he already believes: that the Lord has already broken the enemy's power in his life at baptism. But the Christian must acknowledge that, for some reason, a door has since been opened, giving the enemy some degree of access to his heart and mind. He must actively take his stand against the schemes of the devil (Eph 6), not only by repenting of sin (which most Catholics already understand), but further by *renouncing* any form of agreement with the deceptions of the enemy. In baptism, the Catholic has received the gift of freedom, and through conversion, he has embraced the truth of his baptism. This is the foundational truth on which he can take his stand.

DELIVERANCE IN THE SACRAMENT OF RECONCILIATION

The sacrament of Reconciliation is a renewal of baptism and, therefore, includes deliverance ministry. Deliverance from sin, the world, the flesh, and the devil takes place as we humbly confess our sin and return to the profound encounter with God we have received through baptism and faith. Sacramental confession remains the normal means that God uses to help us deal with sin. But since sin is often hidden behind lies we believe, with no awareness of their falsehood, true contrition is not always possible. In such cases, the Holy Spirit's gift of discernment can lead the priest to insight into the root cause of the lie. The penitent may now be aware of specific mistaken beliefs for which to repent during his next confession, and will have a raised consciousness to recognize and resist the lies to which he had been unhealthily responding. Thus, a pattern or cycle of sin can be broken and healed.

DELIVERANCE IN THE MASS

The Eucharist is a sacrament of healing. In it, we receive Jesus, who not only reveals himself to our eyes of faith but also reveals to us who *we* are. As we receive him and behold his presence, we are transformed into his likeness.

> We all, with unveiled face, beholding the glory of the Lord, are being changed into his likeness from one degree of glory to another.
>
> — 2 Cor 3:18

It's not unusual for someone to come to Mass feeling oppressed, only to experience the oppression lift by the time the priest or deacon tells us, "Go now in peace, to love and serve the Lord." The book of James teaches us that the devil will flee from us, as we resist him and draw near to God:

> Submit yourselves therefore to God. Resist the devil and he will flee from you. Draw near to God and he will draw near to you.
>
> — Jas 4:7-8

By drawing close to God in the Eucharist and resisting temptation, we can experience deliverance from oppression. Deliverance is not just freedom *from* something, but it is freedom *for* knowing the Father, through the Son, in the power of the Holy Spirit. We have this opportunity at every Eucharist. Deliverance is about freedom, the freedom found only in Christ.

Furthermore, as the book of Revelation indicates, those who worship the Father are "full of eyes all round and within" (Rev 4:8). This conveys the spiritual truth that worship grants us the purified ability to see ourselves truly. This is particularly true when we participate in the liturgy, since it is "the source and summit of the Christian life" (*CCC* 1324). We can become aware of false identity, spiritual roots of bondage, and core deceptions, during Mass. This revelation opens the door to deliverance.

DELIVERANCE IN THE PREACHING MINISTRY

God uses preaching to reveal the hidden things of our hearts; he uses preaching to introduce the truth of His love into areas held in darkness. Deliverance comes when the truth exposes lies and our Enemy has no place to hide anymore. The preaching of the Gospel prepares adults for baptism and readies our hearts for the sacrament of Reconciliation.

Years ago, I had the opportunity to be part of an interchurch service in South Philadelphia. I, like other European-Americans there, was especially drawn to the interracial and intercultural worship, but an African-American man I spoke with was most excited by the preaching. "I get set free when the word is preached," he declared to me. We can expect such results from inspired homilies to our own Catholic congregations as well.

Deliverance in Evangelization

Evangelization also involves deliverance ministry, especially when it helps someone make a personal response to the salvation and freedom he has been given in Christ. I remember one young man who was trying to break off an immoral relationship. As he sat on our couch, he said he wanted to be free; he prayed, and he listened to the truth, but ten minutes later, he was overwhelmed with emotions and confusion. We prayed for him to be free of every evil influence, but the fundamental issue was that he had to decide again and again to follow Jesus and be His disciple. There is no substitute for a personal relationship with our Lord. We can't free anyone. It is the Truth, Jesus himself, who sets us free. Jesus will never be content with only being a part of our lives. He wants to *be* our life!

Deliverance in Healing Services

Deliverance goes on during retreats and ministries directed at healing. Healing cannot be separated from deliverance. It is clear in the Scriptures that Jesus never separated the two. He sent His disciples to heal the sick and drive out demons. Rachel's Vineyard, a post-abortion ministry, has designed retreats to bring healing to men and women who are suffering because of their participation in an abortion. Though the retreat is not advertised as deliverance, Theresa Burke, PhD, the founder of Rachel's Vineyard, knows that deliverance is what takes place as the women and men come to the Lord with their sin and their torment.

Praying for Deliverance

Jesus taught us to pray for deliverance. We pray this regularly when we pray the Our Father: "Lead us not into temptation, but deliver us from evil." In the appendix to the new Rite of Exorcism, we are encouraged to pray for deliverance from the evil one. This expression of prayer helps to restore to the people of God a sense of the spiritual realities that surround us in our everyday lives. (It is a serious disadvantage to be in a battle without recognizing the presence of an enemy!) Learning to sincerely ask God for freedom and deliverance, for one another and for ourselves, opens our eyes of faith. Such prayer would enable us to see the reality of the spiritual warfare in which we live. The two kingdoms would no longer be hidden from us. Thus, deliverance should be seen as a normal part of the Christian life.

Deliverance Ministry

Deliverance ministry, then, can encompass all efforts made through prayer, counseling, exhortation, and command to help others gain freedom in areas of spiritual bondage. Recognizing that many activities in the Church qualify as deliverance ministry, I recommend the use of the term *deliverance prayer* for the specific efforts made to help others be rid of demonic influence.

The Lord gives me — and every believer — the privilege of participating in his work because he so desires to set the captives free. As part of the body of Christ, we are to do the things that Jesus did. As the Lord has taught me, so I want to teach others to be an instrument of his love. When we train others in deliverance prayer, we do not teach them how to set up a deliverance ministry with official ramifications. Rather, we simply teach them that all believers have authority over their enemies. Loving others with the power and wisdom God has given us is an expression of the ministry of Jesus and the ministry of the universal Church. The Canticle of Zechariah, prayed daily by the universal Church in the divine office, proclaims:

> Blessed be the Lord God of Israel,
> for he has visited and redeemed his people,
> and has raised up a horn of salvation for us in the
> house of his servant
> David,
> as he spoke by the mouth of his holy prophets from
> of old,
> that we should be saved from our enemies,
> and from the hand of all who hate us;
> to perform the mercy promised to our fathers,
> and to remember his holy covenant,
> the oath which he swore to our father Abraham, to
> grant us
> that we, being delivered from the hand of our enemies,
> might serve him without fear,
> in holiness and righteousness before him all the days
> of our life.
> — Lk 1:68-75

We have spiritual enemies. Deliverance from their influence is part of our inheritance and should be a normal part of the life of every Catholic.

I have already distinguished between confrontational and non-confrontational deliverance models. Within these two basic models is a wide variety in practice. Each ministry may be as unique as its leader. The approach I teach has as its purpose releasing people into the love of the Father, through Jesus Christ, by first setting them free from bondage to evil spirits. Our model looks a lot more like evangelization than it does exorcism.

The Unbound Model

The Unbound Model has been developed over many years of experience and is explained fully in my book *Unbound: a Practical Guide to Deliverance* (2003). A model is something that can be looked at, studied, and replicated. Through the process, the reader will gain understanding, then lay a foundation upon which to build his own model. I teach guidelines on how to use the Unbound Model, and I hope readers will use the guidelines so they can deeply understand them *before* they attempt to combine this model with other approaches.

But there is a distinction between the principles I teach, which are universals, and the way they are applied in ministry. That's why I am hesitant to call the guidelines a method. A method is a way of doing something, a technique — implying that if a minister does this particular thing or prays that particular prayer, people will gain their freedom. However, there is no way to help someone enter into the freedom Jesus has given them apart from the Holy Spirit. We can present the model, but God has to make it work. Little lasting change will come to the one for whom we pray unless we unite our actions and words with the active work of the Holy Spirit, in both our life and the heart of the one for whom we pray. We must have compassion; they must be open to the touch of God. The ministry of Jesus is to set the captives free; we are but His unworthy servants, joining Him in doing what the Father is doing.

The Model Explained

Briefly, the Unbound Model focuses on five keys, which I consider universal to deliverance.

1. The first key is Repentance and Faith. Mark records that when Jesus began his ministry, he came "saying, 'The time is fulfilled, and the kingdom of God is at hand; repent, and believe in the gospel'" (Mk 1:15). This first

key, then, is leading people to make a personal response to the Savior. Pope John Paul II defined conversion as accepting by personal decision the saving sovereignty of Christ and becoming his disciple (*Redemptoris Missio*, 46). This is the foundation of all deliverance. The second aspect of this key is that sins must be turned from and confessed.

2. The second key is Forgiveness. Jesus makes it very clear that our refusal to forgive others blocks us from God's love, which makes us subject to the enemy. The Gospel of Matthew records Jesus' words in the parable of the unforgiving servant:

> "And in anger his lord delivered him to the jailers, till he should pay all his debt. So also my heavenly Father will do to every one of you, if you do not forgive your brother from your heart."
>
> — Mt 18:34-35

3. The third key is Renunciation. Jesus tells us that the devil is the father of lies. When Jesus hung on the cross and said, "Father, forgive them; they do not know what they are doing," he made it clear that every sin contains an element of deception. We must renounce deceptions with which we have identified, with which we have agreed, or which we treated as companions. When we renounce, in the name of Jesus, the specific lies we have adopted as our own, we break the power of those lies in our lives.

4. The fourth key is Authority. We exercise authority by verbally commanding, in the name of Jesus, any spirit we have renounced to leave. Speaking in his holy name reminds us that it is not we who free ourselves, but it is the work of Jesus through us that brings freedom. God has promised us victory over our enemies. We really do

have spiritual enemies, and in Christ we have the victory. We need to know and express the authority that we have. The disciples returned to Jesus after proclaiming the kingdom of God, and rejoiced, saying, "Even the demons submit to us in your name."

5. The final key is The Father's Blessing. We all need a revelation that our true identity is found in God the Father. This is the deepest healing we all seek. In the Father, we discover that we are sons and daughters — children of the eternal God, the Father of Jesus.

> See what love the Father has given us, that we should be called children of God; and so we are.
>
> — 1 Jn 3:1

In ministry using the Unbound Model, we pray for this revelation for the ones to whom we minister, because we know that God wants to pour his love into each of his children by the Holy Spirit (Rom 5:5). Once spiritual obstacles are removed, the love of God will come rushing in. As we receive understanding of their true identity, we are able to declare confidently that God has a purpose and plan for them. And we are able to speak into each heart this truth: Jesus, the Son, dwells in you, and the blessing that the Father spoke to Jesus at his baptism belongs to you as well.

> You are my son / You are my daughter, whom I love, and with you I am well pleased.
>
> (See Mk 1:11)

Using the framework of these keys, we teach people to listen to another's story. We are not giving advice or catechesis. Rather, we listen carefully, looking in these five keys for the place in their story where the victory of Jesus has yet to be applied. We help each individual take her stand, resist the devil's power, and respond to the Lord.

WHERE DOES THE DEVIL GET HIS POWER?

In the beginning, the devil had no access or power on the earth. God gave Adam and Eve the authority to rule the earth as his representatives. The devil could only gain access within the parameters that God had established. He would have to do it through the man and the woman. In the garden, there was but one "do not":

> "Of the tree of the knowledge of good and evil you shall not eat, for in the day that you eat of it you shall die."

— Gen 2:17

If the devil could draw the man and woman out from this intimate relationship with God as his son and daughter, he could gain access and exert influence. He wanted what God had — children and a kingdom, through which he could oppose God. To get that authority, he would have to get it from us.

Through sin, Adam and Eve broke the only law that God gave. Prior to their sin, they didn't live under the law but above the law, fulfilling the desires of God simply by giving back to God the love he gave to them. The devil is a legalist; he operates based on the law. In Jesus, we fulfill the law and therefore are not subject to the devil. It is only when we live apart from the Son of God that we are subject to the enemy. Understanding that the devil can only be active in our lives if he has legitimate access is the basis for understanding how we are set free through the Gospel.

We can learn to help others cancel the devil's access and close the door to him without confronting the evil spirits. When we close the devil's entryway, there should be no need for a spirit to manifest. Even if a confrontational model is used, or there is a demonic manifestation at some level, the entryway must always be addressed for the person to be set free and to continue to walk in his freedom.

Do You Need Deliverance?

Considering the simplicity of the five keys, the emphasis on listening, and the context of evangelization, how many of the 400 people who called Fr. Francis last year would have benefited from deliverance ministry, including the two who needed exorcism? I cannot answer that question, because, ultimately, the only help that we can give comes from God. We, like Jesus, can only do what the Father is doing.

But in another respect, we can say *all* would have benefited from a personal encounter with Jesus and from help surrendering to God. *All* would have benefited from deeper conviction of sin. *All* would have benefited from seeing how deception is so intertwined with their sinful responses in life, and how both deception and sin are connected to what is troubling them. *All* would have benefited from this preparation for a humble and honest confession. *All* would have benefited from exposing the lies that have compromised their utter reliance on God as their Father.

Although it is very unlikely that you need an exorcism, deliverance from the influence of evil spirits is certainly part of what God has for you. The difference between deliverance ministry and exorcism — or a style of deliverance ministry that looks like exorcism — is like the difference between surgery and physical therapy.

One has surgery when he has unsuccessfully tried everything else. The surgeon puts the patient to sleep and deals with the problem. He doesn't do it without the patient's consent or help, without careful diagnostic work — and he shouldn't do it unless all else has failed. It is a last resort.

On the other hand, deliverance is like physical therapy. In physical therapy, the therapist comes alongside the patient, teaches him, and empowers him do what he needs to do. It is easier to train a physical therapist than it is to train a surgeon.

I had back surgery in 1984. The surgery was not a big success until I began a good program of physical therapy and a serious strengthening program that I continue today. Now, I know that if I had a good physical therapy program in the first place, I may not have needed to go through the surgery.

Do you need deliverance? Let me ask a better question. Do you need evangelization? Do you need to take deeper hold of the freedom you have been given in Christ? Is there a battle you need to fight? You have been given the weapons.

> For the weapons of our warfare are not of the flesh but have divine power to destroy strongholds.
> — 1 Cor 10:4

As we learn to use all the weapons in God's armory, we will increasingly find the freedom Christ won for us and the purpose he holds for us.

Chapter 4

Reclaiming Our Lost Weapons of Spiritual Warfare

> But if it is by the Spirit of God that I cast out demons,
> then the Kingdom of God has come upon you.
>
> — Mt 12:28

If we are to make use of the weapons God has provided for fighting evil, we must know what they are. In addition to the defensive armor listed by Paul, Ephesians 6 admonishes us:

> In all circumstances, take up the shield of faith with which you can extinguish all the flaming darts of the evil one; and take the helmet of salvation and the sword of the Spirit which is the word of God, praying at all times in the Spirit with all prayer and supplication.
>
> — Eph 6:16-18a

What does it mean to pray "in the Spirit"? Does how we pray matter, really? Well, yes, it does. Eugene Peterson paraphrases St. Paul's concern well in *The Message*, when he writes:

> This is no afternoon athletic contest that we'll walk away from and forget about in a couple of hours. This is for keeps; a life-or-death fight to the finish against the Devil and all his angels.
>
> — Eph 6:12

The seriousness of our fight and its eternal consequences lead St. Paul to remind us that our greatest weapons come by the Spirit of Jesus Christ.

Jesus drove out spirits by the Spirit of God; he sent his disciples out, empowering them to do the same, by the same

Spirit. When he sent out the seventy[16] disciples as recorded in Luke 10, he sent them out saying:

> Whenever you enter a town and they receive you, eat what is set before you; heal the sick in it and say to them, "The kingdom of God has come near to you."

The healing of the sick and the casting out of demons were linked together as bodies were made whole and the inner man was liberated from demonic torment. The seventy returned to Jesus after a mission of proclaiming the kingdom of God, declaring, "Even the demons submit to us in your name."

A gift given by the Spirit empowering us to share in Christ's mission is called a charism. The word *charism* is from the Greek term used by St. Paul meaning "favor," "gratuitous gift," or "benefit" (*CCC* 2003). It is the term used for the special graces that Paul describes in 1 Corinthians 12:10. Many Catholics may be familiar with the Church's use of the term *charism* to describe a particular religious order's spirituality or specific emphasis, such as the Benedictines' particular charism of hospitality. But here, I shall instead be using the term *charism* in its Pauline sense.

Charisms are the perennial expression of the one gift of the Spirit given at Pentecost. They are not gifts that we possess to keep for personal gain, but are gifts that are made evident in our lives *as we yield our lives* to the Holy Spirit *with expectant faith.* They are "workings" of the Spirit, who continues the mission of Jesus in his followers, advancing the Kingdom of God.

Charisms build up the Church and advance the common good. Some people are given the gift to prophesy, some to serve, some to teach, some to encourage, and some to give generously. There are many other graces given by the Spirit as well, which the Apostle Paul mentions in Romans 12 and 1 Corinthians 12. The Spirit bestows these graces as he wills, wherever and whenever he finds believers open to them. He chooses to use some people regularly with certain gifts. But we cannot possess these gifts apart from the indwelling of the Spirit that has been given to us in baptism and activated by faith. It is only to the extent that we allow the Spirit of God to "possess" us that it is appropriate to think of spiritual gifts being in our possession.

When a charism is at work, people recognize that something special, beyond human talent, has been revealed. There is the sense of the supernatural. When charisms are active, it is easy to recognize that God is in the midst of His people. Love, manifested in those who serve, comes from a deeper source than simply their own hearts. Words of prophecy bring personalized encouragement that comes from the heart of God and profoundly resonates with our deepest need. Healing power is released to heal the inner wounds and restore the body. Wisdom, evident in those who listen to the heart of God, comes from above their rational minds. This recognition of the supernatural displayed through ordinary people builds and ignites our faith. After experiencing these charisms, we are now able to ask God for what we need with increased confidence. As a body of believers, we are able, now, to ask that the Spirit advance the Church's mission, and have assurance that he will do it. Our access to the power of the Holy Spirit through the charisms is a most powerful weapon against evil, and is something every Catholic believer carries through his baptism and the activation of his faith.

Loss of Charisms

Charisms are Jesus' gift to his Church. In the earliest days of the Church, Christians rejoiced in both the ordinary and the extraordinary signs of the Spirit working among them. They depended on the Holy Spirit for personal guidance and direction, rather than on an institutionalized office. Yet over time, charisms began to be lost to the Christian layperson and reserved exclusively for those in office. Some charisms were lost altogether.

In their book *Christian Initiation and baptism in the Holy Spirit*, Fr. Killian McDonnell and Fr. George Montague point to four reasons why charisms began to be severed from the life of the Church.[17] These are the increasing prevalence of infant baptism, the reaction to Montanism, the shift toward viewing charisms as signs of holiness, and the establishment of hierarchal power. Let me briefly summarize why each of those led to the loss of charisms in the modern Church.

1. In the early Church, there was a lively expectation for an outpouring of spiritual power and the release of charisms at baptism. As a candidate underwent lengthy preparation, he approached baptism with a great expectation for the transforming power of the Holy Spirit and the release of charisms, which would empower him to serve the Lord and his Church. This changed when infant baptism became the norm. A primary focus for the release and use of charisms was removed, leading to their diminished use.

2. Montanism was a second-century movement marked by prophecy and other charisms. At the time, it was referred to as the "New Prophecy." Montanism tended to be anti-hierarchical. Because of the manner in which the prophecies were delivered, and because of abuses of the charisms, Montanism was later condemned. The prophetic charism was still important to the Church at this time, and St. Irenaeus warned that steps taken to prevent false prophecy might result in rejecting prophecy altogether.[18] St. Irenaeus was correct. With the condemnation of Montanism, prophecy soon lost its place in the Church and even the word *prophet* slowly disappeared from the normal Christian life.[19] It is possible that the enemy used Montanism — which came from Phrygia, a center for pagan ecstatic religion — as a diabolical influence to corrupt true prophecy and its place in the Church.

3. The charisms continued to be demonstrated through time in the holiest of people — the saints. The general belief developed that charisms were rare and extraordinary signs of holiness. For a regular Christian to seek the gift of healing, for example, was interpreted as a prideful desire, rather than seen correctly as a compassionate desire to see others healed and the Gospel advanced.[20]

4. As the Church grew, and the end of history no longer seemed so near, the responsibility for unity grew. The Tradition of the apostles had to be defended against false teaching. The witness of Scripture and Tradition acquired greater weight and importance. One of the main duties of the developing hierarchy in the Church was to serve and preserve Tradition and the body of truth it contained.[21] This fight for unity, as well as the battle against heresy and abuse, shifted from the local communities — where charisms were active — toward established Church office. Through the centuries, the sense of the "workings" of the Spirit through individuals, or groups, apart from ordained leaders decreased. All of the charisms suffered.

BELIEVERS FORGET THEIR AUTHORITY AND MANDATE

The charism of casting out spirits, in particular, was lost from the life of the average Christian as the Church increasingly reserved the exercise of this gift for the ordained or the holy. Over time, the charism of driving out spirits became identified solely with exorcism. This is unfortunate as well as unnecessary. Jesus came to liberate captives and deliver prisoners from darkness (Is 61:2). And that is what all his followers, in his name, are called to do today (Mk 16:17).

Jesus' exorcisms, says Fr. Jeffrey Grob, "were utterly simple, merely commanding the demons to depart. No physical device, no incantation, no proof of departure was required. These demonic encounters were all taken as indications that the Kingdom of God was at hand."[22] Another way of saying it is that in Jesus, heaven was touching earth. As Jesus passed his ministry on to the ancient Church, says Grob, every Christian was able to exercise this ministry, using "Jesus' name and the power it conveyed." St. Justin Martyr wrote in the second century that "many of our Christian men exorcising [numberless demoniacs] throughout the whole world in the name of Jesus Christ . . . have healed and do heal, rendering helpless and driving the possessing devils out of the men, though they could not be cured by all the other exorcists, and those who used incantations and drugs."[23]

Though some still use *exorcism* to describe any action that is used to drive out evil spirits, the terms *deliverance* and *liberation* better distinguish between the use of charisms to help people overcome the bondage to the enemy and the sacred Rite of Exorcism.[24] All believers in Jesus can and should participate at some level in delivering or liberating others from spiritual bondage. Why, then, has the Church lost this simple ministry?

Fr. Grob, in reflecting on the loss of the charism of casting out demons, places blame on abuse:

> All Christians potentially possessed the special Charism needed to expel demons by virtue of their baptism. This, at any rate, was the case until the third and fourth centuries when an order of exorcists began to emerge in some parts of the Church.[25] Whereas before, the work of the exorcist was seen as a universal gift granted to all believers by God, now it was becoming an appointment by the Church. What was once a function rapidly became a title and an office. What brought about that change? . . . Through a need to institutionalize the practice of exorcism and out of concern brought on by the abuses of exorcists and unbelievers, the future of exorcism was restricted to an office held either by ordination or appointment.[26]

Abuses were plentiful. There were those who wanted to make money through deliverance. Some even paraded "possessed" persons and charged money as the demons were challenged and the evil spirits were driven to manifest. There were times when fear and superstition were rampant in the Church, leading multitudes to look for exorcism. In response to abuses, the Church developed the order of exorcist, which eventually led to the first Rite of Exorcism in 1614.

The order of exorcist provided a means by which the Church could officially, and publically, respond to the needs of the truly possessed. But the Church did not establish the order of exorcist for the purpose of eliminating the practice of deliverance by lay people. No, the exorcist order was instituted to bring order to the ministry of the Church and to give the charisms a form for expression. Unfortunately — as we saw earlier — just as when the Church moved to infant baptism and did not replace the framework for the expression of charisms, so in this case, the framework for the expression of the charism of casting out spirits was removed and was not replaced by another form. The laity no longer freely exercised this important charism. The Catholic believer lost his familiarity with, and his daily use of, the weapons with "divine power to destroy strongholds" (2 Cor. 10:4).

It is not uncommon now for Christians to struggle with the same sin patterns and issues year after year. In the midst of such struggle, many Catholics have little or no expectation of release. Many think, as I once did, that their lot in life is to struggle through and not mess up, all so they can get to Heaven. The desire to spend eternity with God should affect us at every level of our lives, but God has also given us a purpose to fulfill on earth. When we have low expectations of spiritual power, because we are not exercising the charisms, we are robbed of the life the Lord intended us to live; we are robbed of our purpose.

Jesus tirelessly proclaimed the Kingdom, speaking transforming words into people's lives. He revealed the Father in his words and actions, as he healed the sick and drove out demons. The words of Jesus to his disciples are spoken to us as well: "As the Father has sent me, so I am sending you." The only way for us to fulfill this mandate of our Lord is to go in the power of his Spirit.

REGAINING LOST CHARISMS

I grew up with the impression that it was the role of the laity to pray and obey and to let the real serving be done by the clergy. This is not surprising. Catholics have all the benefits of the sacrament of Reconciliation, the Rite of Exorcism, and the Anointing of the Sick by which those in need would be served. But these gifts were never intended to suppress the workings of the Spirit through ordinary believers. For the first three hundred years of the Church, ordinary Christians cast out spirits by the name of Jesus and the Spirit of God. Origen (AD 203-250) recorded the commonplace nature of the charism of casting out demons when he wrote:

> And [the casting out of demons], we may observe, they do without the use of any curious arts of magic, or incantations, but merely by prayer and simple adjurations which the plainest person can use. Because for the most part it is unlettered persons who perform this work; thus making manifest the grace which is in the word of Christ, and the despicable weakness of demons, which, in order to be overcome and driven out of the bodies and souls of men, do not require the power and wisdom of those who are mighty in argument, and most learned in matters of faith.[27]

The loss of this activity did not signal growth or a higher level of development, but impoverishment. The Church must regain the charisms, and with them the power of living and praying by the Spirit, for people to become whole. The tremendous beauty of even one Christian set free is unforgettably amazing. How much more beautiful, inspiring, and fruitful would be the release of hundreds, even thousands, of souls to freedom!

Because of the incredible graciousness of God, I received the Spirit as an infant when I was baptized. I had no faith of my own, but God looked on the faith of the Church and my parents and godparents. Throughout my life, the Spirit has influenced me, protected me, and provided for me in ways I will never fully comprehend. Through it all, he was working everything for my good (Rom 8:28).

When I was twenty-one years old, I had an experience of the release of the Spirit. In an instant, I knew that God was real and that Jesus had indeed risen from the dead. He was alive and my life meant something. I now had a purpose. I know now that God prepared me for that moment. This encounter with God was only the beginning of a life of ongoing transformation. I had to learn that God was using hardships, conflicts, disappointments, and trouble of various kinds to do something deep in me. My story is not unique. For any of us, moments of personal encounter with the love of God release power to transform us into the likeness of the Son.

If you are reading this book because you are having trouble and looking for answers, there is no greater answer than the love of God manifested in the revelation of Jesus though the Holy Spirit. Victory over areas of bondage — or even serious demonic possession — has one ultimate purpose: to set you free to enter fully into the heart of the Father and know his love through the Son.

Conversion begins with the action of God in our hearts. Jesus tells us in John 6:44, "No one can come to me unless the Father who sent me draws him." The Father's drawing our hearts is not limited to his working within us; he also draws us by working through the Church and circumstances. Faith comes from hearing, say the Scriptures. I may be really ready to respond to

God, but if I am not told of his love or his power, how do I receive the transforming Word? To what truth do I surrender? In order for our baptism to flower into fruitful life, we need both the message and the faith:

> For good news came to us just as to them; but the message which they heard did not benefit them, because it did not meet with faith in the hearers.
>
> — Heb 4:2

The words of Scripture provide the message; we receive faith through a personal encounter with the Son of God. Whether it occurs during prayer, in the reception of the sacraments, or during an extraordinary meeting with Jesus, every encounter with God is meant to change us. His love revealed changes everything.

With conversion comes power. With conversion comes not only the power to be transformed but also the power to help advance the Kingdom of God. Yes, God wants to be released in us, but he wants so much more than that. He wants to be released *through* us.

The Holy Spirit was working in and through Jesus to drive out spirits and advance the Kingdom that he announced. When the Spirit manifests himself through us for the sake of others, we are exercising a charism. Although we are immeasurably blessed to have God work through us, these charisms are not for our benefit but for the benefit of others. They build up the Church, serve others, and advance the Kingdom of God by bringing light into dark and empty spaces. There is nothing more exciting than living a life filled with personal freedom and purpose. To make known the love of God, to offer revelation, encouragement, wisdom, and guidance to those who hurt, to help another find freedom in Christ — all these make life meaningful.

Releasing the Holy Spirit

If you have never heard this message before, it is likely that you do not exercise a charism of the Holy Spirit very often. Yet it is never too late. My brother John is a permanent deacon who offers parish missions. He often hears comments like those he received at his last mission. A man came up to him with tears in his eyes saying, "I am 65 years old, I have been going to church for 60 years, and tonight was the first time I experienced God in a personal way in my life."

You may say, "I want that deeper life," but you may not know how the Spirit of God is released. Start by doing whatever it takes to develop an expectation for a transforming encounter with God. Ask God to work through you by His Spirit. Find others who have been transformed by their relationship with God and join them in their journey of faith. We know that the Spirit is released in us in three ways — by faith, hearing, and seeking. Faith is a gift from God that empowers us to respond to the revelation of God in Jesus Christ and all the truth that was hidden in him from the beginning. Faith comes by hearing. What story were you told about God? Were you told about an old man in heaven waiting to judge you? Or were you told about the broken heart of the Father who sent his Son to save you from your sin? Were you told of our God who thinks you are so unique that he has designed a plan for your life that only you can fulfill?

Finally, the Spirit is released by "knocking" and seeking:

> "If you, then, who are evil, know how to give good gifts to your children, how much more will the heavenly Father give the Holy Spirit to those who ask him!"
> — Lk 11:13

It is in the midst of hardship that we seek God, and it is there that we decide to trust him. At the very place where our will is opposed, we learn to surrender to him fully. At that place, the Lord will release his Spirit with power in our lives in a way that spills over to bless the lives of those around us. We were created for such intimacy with *each* Person of the Trinity. Let us not allow custom or fear of the unknown to rob us of our inheritance.

New Vitality in the Church

After centuries of disuse of the charisms among the laity of the Church, it is not surprising that the renewed expressions of charisms have caused some tension in the Church. Among other things, Church authorities are responsible for good order, for appropriate liturgy, and for the teaching of universal practice and belief. Sometimes our leaders, successors of the Apostles though they are, might be uncomfortable by the claims that God is using lay people apart from the current structure of ministry. That may lead them to minimize the importance of certain charisms. Suspicion, criticism, and alienation are not uncommon occurrences in any of us who bear the fallen human nature. Pope Benedict XVI, however, in addressing bishops and representatives of ecclesial movements and new communities, recognized the importance of having the charisms restored to the Church, saying that we have:

> . . . the important task of promoting a more mature communion of all the ecclesial elements, so that all the charisms, with respect for their specificity, may freely and fully contribute to the edification of the one Body of Christ.[28]

The Holy Father also noted that the growth of the use of charisms in the ecclesial movements and new communities in the Church had brought new life and power into the Catholic experience.

> Paul VI and John Paul II were able to welcome and discern, to encourage and promote the unexpected explosion

of the new lay realities which in various and surprising forms have restored vitality, faith, and hope to the whole Church.

Those who exercise the charisms given to them by the Lord have truly added much to the life of the Church.

We have witnessed the reawakening of a vigorous missionary impetus, motivated by the desire to communicate to all the precious experience of the encounter with Christ, felt and lived as the only adequate response to the human heart's profound thirst for truth and happiness.

Pope Benedict XVI expressed, in this address, what many Catholics have experienced: that the release of the Holy Spirit in an individual life, as well as in the Church at large, will bring victory and power back to the human heart.

As a father of four sons, it is my delight to see in them greatness which goes beyond anything I have ever touched in my life. Though they often thought they were ready for responsibility and privileges long before I thought they were, though there were times they messed up and plenty of times that I did, I recognized that as a father, I had to believe and to trust. I had to let them fall and get up. It was my role to teach and guide so that they might find in God the power to boldly take hold of their calling to serve. In the same way, the Church, in her role as Mother, is called to trust the work of the Holy Spirit in the lives of her children. The Church has always had the responsibility of raising Christians to maturity — to be disciples ready to take up the gifts given to them and to use them to work for the Kingdom, in cooperation and unity with the rest of the Church.

DRINK DEEPLY

A missionary told me a story about the garden he had planted. He gave one of his employees the task of watering the plants, but each day the plants seemed to deteriorate a little more. They sagged and wilted; they turned yellow. Finally, the missionary asked the man if he had filled the bucket and taken it to the garden.

"Yes sir," the man answered.

"Show me what you are doing," the missionary said.

He went with him as the man filled the bucket and walked it over to the garden. He watched his employee carefully place the bucket on the dirt in the garden. The man stood up and turned away. He never released the water by pouring it into the dry soil so the plants could drink.

We have been given the water of life — the Holy Spirit. It is a great thing to know we have received him at baptism, but it is another thing to drink deeply of him so that every part of us can soak in the love of God. It is one thing to know that God has promised that from us would flow fountains of living water; it is another thing to experience those waters going out from us toward those that are dry and thirsty for the love of God.

We believe that we have the Spirit through baptismal faith. We know there is power in the sacraments. What we still need to do is release that power to have access to what is already present. The water is in the bucket; it won't take much to tip it over. Once the bucket is tipped over and the water flows out, we will have the strength to fight the powers of this dark world and put them to flight.

> Finally, be strong in the Lord and in the strength of his might. Put on the whole armor of God, that you may be able to stand against the wiles of the devil.
>
> — Eph 6:10-11

CHAPTER 5

Exorcism and Deliverance in the New Testament

That evening they brought to him many who were possessed with demons; and he cast out the spirits with a word, and healed all who were sick.

— Mt 8:16

The entire ministry of Jesus on earth could be characterized as a deliverance ministry. As the Holy Father emphasized in his book, *Jesus of Nazareth*, Jesus was the new Moses, leading the people out of bondage and into the Promised Land. Just as God had destroyed Pharaoh's enslaving power through Moses, God now destroys the power of the devil through Jesus. Healing the sick and casting out spirits characterized both Jesus' ministry and that of the disciples he sent out. In Luke 10, the disciples came back from a mission with great rejoicing. "Even the demons submit to us," they said. The importance of driving out spirits must not be minimized. After the disciples reported what they had seen, Jesus rejoiced in the Holy Spirit and declared:

"Blessed are the eyes which see what you see! For I tell you that many prophets and kings desired to see what you see, and did not see it, and to hear what you hear, and did not hear it."

— Lk 10:23-24

Exorcism — in fact, every effort that specifically seeks to set people free from the influence of evil spirits — traces directly back to the ministry of Jesus. With these New Testament accounts, we can measure and test current practices, and evaluate whether they are consistent with Jesus' ministry.

THE KINGDOM

The New Testament does not explicitly refer to Jesus as a "healer" or an "exorcist." He simply healed the sick, cast out demons, and raised the dead as an expression of the message of the Kingdom of God that he proclaimed. The Kingdom is the reign of God, or, as Pope Benedict describes it, God's lordship.[29] But Jesus didn't merely proclaim the message of the Kingdom. He made the Kingdom present by his actions. The presence of the Light of the world exposed the darkness. Jesus ushered the Kingdom into this world that was under the dominion of Satan. At the beginning of Jesus' public ministry, he boldly read from Isaiah:

> The Spirit of the Lord is upon me, because he has anointed me to preach good news to the poor. He has sent me to proclaim release to the captives and recovering of sight to the blind, to set at liberty those who are oppressed, to proclaim the acceptable year of the Lord.
>
> — Lk 4:18-19

Jesus invites us to enter into his very mission of proclaiming the Kingdom and living the life of the Kingdom. His ministry now continues by the power of the Holy Spirit in us. It would make little sense for us to preach liberty for the oppressed, unless the message actually carried the power to procure freedom. For all in bondage of any sort, the Good News is validated by the power it has to set us free. Bondage may take the form of unbelief or compulsive sin; internal accusations of worthlessness or meaninglessness; uncontrollable thoughts of self-hatred, self-rejection, or bitterness; or a host of other issues. Like the supernatural healing of the sick, the driving out of spirits validates the message of Jesus in our lives. The New Testament demonstrates the reality of the coming Kingdom in Jesus that will be made fully present in the future, as we pray the way the Lord taught us: "Thy kingdom come; Thy will be done on earth as it is in heaven."

Jesus healed all those oppressed by the devil who came to him.[30] But we have only a handful of detailed accounts of deliverance relative to the numbers of people who came to him. Therefore, we cannot analyze all the ways people were delivered from lesser degrees of bondage. As we have seen, there are differing degrees even under what is labeled "possession." We've distinguished between possession and complete possession, as well as oppression and obsession. What we do know is that in Jesus we have the Kingdom of God breaking into our world, and we can see in the ministry of Jesus the principles that are foundational to every level of both exorcism and deliverance ministry. As we look at several New Testament passages, we are looking for these foundational principles.

CHALLENGING UNBELIEF IN THE SPIRIT'S WORK

As Jesus carried out his Father's mission, he proclaimed the message of the Kingdom, healed the sick, and cast out demons. One day, his actions evoked a strong response from the religious leaders. In Matthew 12:22-37, we read about a blind and dumb man whom Jesus healed by casting out a spirit that was mute (see also Lk 11:14-26). The people were amazed. "Can this be the Son of David?" they said. Their reaction was a threat to the Pharisees, the local religious authorities, who responded differently. "It is only by Beelzebub, the prince of demons, that this man casts out demons," they said. Though Jesus did not hear their remarks, he knew their thoughts and pointed out the foolishness of their argument:

> Every kingdom divided against itself is laid waste, and no city or house divided against itself will stand; and if Satan casts out Satan, he is divided against himself; how then will his kingdom stand? And if I cast out demons by Beelzebub, by whom do your sons cast them out? Therefore they shall be your judges.
>
> — Mt 12:25b-27

Jesus acknowledged that the Jews had the means to cast out spirits. In Acts 19, we read about itinerant Jewish exorcists who were part of the religious culture of that day. The records of these exorcisms indicate that they involved a formula of recitation of names, or what may be described as a ritual, involving actions and words that set the person free from bondage to an evil spirit.[31]

The problem Jesus presented is that he did not cast the spirit out in the manner then considered acceptable by the Jewish leaders. He did not depend on ritual or ceremony; he radically departed from the norm, declaring:

> But if it is by the Spirit of God that I cast out demons, then the kingdom of God has come upon you.
>
> — Mt 12:28

Jesus cast out demons by the Spirit of God on His own authority. Even more significant — the Kingdom of Heaven, the realm of God's rule, came upon those who were set free. When Jesus cast out spirits in a public way, something big took place. Anyone witnessing the deliverance had the same opportunity to have the realm of the Kingdom come upon him. To further demonstrate that he worked by the Spirit of God, Jesus explained that if he was going to rob Satan of what he has stolen, he must first bind him so he could take back what had been stolen. How could he drive a demon out by Beelzebub? That would mean Satan would have to bind himself.

This episode is found in both the Gospel of Luke and that of Matthew. Following each account, we have some very important, but different, statements of Jesus recorded for us. In Matthew's Gospel, Jesus says:

> He who is not with me is against me, and he who does not gather with me scatters. Therefore I tell you, every sin and blasphemy will be forgiven men, but the blasphemy

against the Spirit will not be forgiven. And whoever
says a word against the Son of man will be forgiven;
but whoever speaks against the Holy Spirit will not be
forgiven, either in this age or in the age to come.

— Mt 12:30-32

Jesus does not appear to be personally offended, but he does
take offense on behalf of the Holy Spirit. Not liking Jesus, and
speaking ill of him, are acts and attitudes from which a man may
turn again toward God; but if we see the Spirit of God working
through Jesus and yet declare that what God has done is of the
devil, we are hardening our hearts against our only hope. We
are preventing the Holy Spirit and the Kingdom of God from
breaking into our lives.

Right now, the Kingdom is being manifest to us in a way
that prophets and kings longed to see. This is the moment of our
salvation. The unforgivable sin is to reject the action of the Holy
Spirit that has manifested the Kingdom in a decisive way for our
salvation. There is no middle ground: if we are not an instrument
of the Kingdom, recognizing that the only solution to our deepest
needs is found in Jesus, then we are in opposition to the Kingdom.

The Holy Spirit has always worked in and through Jesus;
they are one, just as Jesus and the Father are one. But in a healing
such as the one in Matthew 12, the Spirit tangibly demonstrated
what Jesus verbally proclaimed. The Kingdom came upon
anyone who accepted the healing or deliverance as being done
by the hand of God.

Jesus once said the Kingdom belonged to the children, the
little ones. Children freely came to Jesus and accepted him. To
be like a child means to come from our lowly position and freely
accept the reign of God, the Lordship of the Almighty. Whose
sin will not be forgiven? Those who, like the Pharisees, hang
onto their blindness in order to oppose the revelation of the
Kingdom will not be forgiven.

The Pharisees were sternly warned by Jesus against this unforgiveable sin. In refusing to see God, they revealed that their religious control was more important to them than the Lord's lordship. This was the day of their salvation, "the great and terrible Day of the Lord," and they were missing it. The driving out of evil spirits was a demonstration and revelation of the Kingdom ushered in by the Spirit though Jesus, the Son of God, a unique opportunity to see and yield to the power of God.

SUBMITTING TO THE LORD'S LORDSHIP

Luke puts Jesus' warning about the seriousness of rejecting the work of the Spirit in a different context in his Gospel (Lk 12:10). But here, in his account of the healing the mute boy, he gives us Jesus' criticism of the way the Jews handled exorcisms. Jesus makes it clear that his way is far superior.

> When the unclean spirit has gone out of a man, he passes through waterless places seeking rest; and finding none he says, 'I will return to my house from which I came.' And when he comes he finds it swept and put in order. Then he goes and brings seven other spirits more evil than himself, and they enter and dwell there; and the last state of that man becomes worse than the first.
>
> — Lk 11:24-26

When Jesus cast out spirits by the Spirit of God, the house, or person, was not left empty, for the Kingdom came upon the one healed. In contrast, when their "sons" cast out spirits, the house was left empty and more demons returned, leaving the once-delivered man in a worse state. It is worth emphasizing again the response that Jesus gives in both Gospels to the attack on his ministry.

> But if it is by the finger (Spirit) of God that I cast out demons, then the Kingdom of God has come upon you.
>
> — Lk 11:20/Mt 12:28

Implicitly, Jesus recognized that there may be various ways to drive a spirit out. His warning is that the expulsion of the demon is incomplete unless the Kingdom comes into the person. The "Lord's lordship" must be present. If the person who has been delivered has not embraced the Kingdom, then a door is left open to the enemy that can lead to an even greater form of bondage or torment.

The enemy's "return" is never pretty. For example, if the Truth does not replace the bondage, the relief at the deliverance may soon give way to more condemnation, perhaps adding hopelessness, helplessness, despair, and even thoughts of suicide. Deliverance opens the inner person to the revelation of God's love and truth.

In Romans 12, we are told that we are transformed by the renewal of our minds. The grace of deliverance brings liberation not only to one's spirit, but also to one's mind. It frees patterns of thought that have been imprisoned, releasing them to be renewed, which leads to a transformed life. As Catholics, we understand that each person is an integrated whole; we find this to be true: when God sets a penitent free spiritually, his emotions, his mind, and his body are soon set free as well. "You will know the truth and the truth will set you free" (Jn 8:32). If we reject any part of the truth of the Kingdom, we may close the door to the transforming power of his love.

Randy struggled with homosexuality. During a time of ministry, he renounced spirits binding him to a homosexual identity and they were driven away. He felt normal for the first time in his life and publicly testified to his deliverance. But the homosexual urges returned and Randy became more hopeless and helpless than ever, wondering what he did wrong or why God had abandoned him. The problem was that the foundation — the internal structure — was not healed and brought under the lordship of Jesus through the redemption of his life's hurts.

Scientists say that nature abhors a vacuum. It is the same with human nature; if we are not filled with the Kingdom, something else will fill us.

At other times, the same spirit does not return, but the very process of deliverance may have left the wounded one open to an alternative deception through which the enemy works. For example, Betty had gone through deliverance sessions complete with manifestations and, as a result, found relief. But the humiliation and trauma of the event left her with a skewed picture of the sovereignty of God and of her position as his daughter. The memory of the devil's power and presence made her glad that she was delivered, but also made her resolve never to go there again. Like a friend of mine who could graphically describe her pain after her surgery, and swore she would go to her grave before having that surgery again, Betty's experience with manifestations during deliverance left her with fear and denial. She was held back from pursuing deeper freedom.

Most people receive deliverance ministry in the context of seeking the Lord, wanting to be his disciple, and desiring to walk in victory over their enemies. They have the same protection found in the New Testament: the protection of Jesus, who reveals the Kingdom. However, if deliverance ministry takes place outside of the context of evangelization and the Lordship of Jesus, the door is left open for the return of the enemy. If deliverance takes place by the Spirit of God and by the authority of Christ, then the Kingdom has come; the "house" is full, and there truly is nothing to fear.

Clearly, Jesus broke with the form of exorcism current among the Jews. In the story recorded in Matthew and Luke, I find three guiding principles that are vital to evaluating the practice of exorcism and deliverance ministry today.

1. Jesus cast out spirits by his own authority. Therefore, his followers do it in his name.

2. Jesus cast out demons by the Spirit.

3. His message was the Kingdom of God, and when he drove out spirits, the Kingdom came upon those who were set free.

Whether deliverance is done through ritual prayer or not, these elements need to be present if we, as his disciples, are imitating the Master. As we look more closely at the healings of Jesus, we will glean more guiding principles to inform our own lives.

GETTING AT THE ROOT

Jesus was obviously very successful at casting out spirits. There was never a failure on his part to help someone who came to him. He drove evil spirits out with a word, revealing that he carried the authority of his Father (Mt 8:16). He was also consistent in the way he drove out spirits. When a spirit manifested in his presence, he commanded it to go. On certain occasions, he would even do a mini "interview," or ask personal background questions.

One day, Jesus' disciples were unable to heal a boy of a dumb and deaf spirit that caused him to seize as if with epilepsy. Desperate, the father brought him to Jesus. As soon as the spirit in the boy saw Jesus, it caused the boy to fall on the ground in a seizure. Jesus turned to the father and asked him, "How long has he had this?" (Mk 9:21).

Since Jesus asked the question in the process of setting the boy free, we can presume it was important. The question leads us to some interesting reflection. The father's answer was "from childhood." This response might have confirmed for Jesus that the entryway for the spirit had to do with his family relationships, and this question led the father into a personal encounter with Jesus.

"And it has often cast him into the fire and into the water, to destroy him; but if you can do anything, have pity on us and help us." And Jesus said to him, "If you can! All things are possible to him who believes." Immediately the father of the child cried out and said, "I believe; help my unbelief!"

— Mk 9:22-24

Jesus challenged the man's faith; he responded by crying out, "I believe; help my unbelief!" Once the father personally appealed to Jesus for himself, the boy was released. Was the enemy's pathway to the boy through the father? Was there something in the father that needed to be addressed before the boy could be set free and remain free? Of course, Jesus could have cast the demon out without the dialogue, but he did not. He was led by the Holy Spirit in the same way we must be.

Asking questions opens the door for the Holy Spirit to shed light on the entryway that needs to be addressed. I have found that if a child is being prayed with for deliverance, the family must be helped as well. For those who are no longer children, forgiveness in relationship to parents is often the key that unlocks the door to freedom. Jesus rebuked the spirit and the boy's torment was over; he went from such a radical state of uncontrolled manifestations of evil to such an intense place of peace that they thought he was dead.

And when Jesus saw that a crowd came running together, he rebuked the unclean spirit, saying to it, "You dumb and deaf spirit, I command you, come out of him, and never enter him again." And after crying out and convulsing him terribly, it came out, and the boy was like a corpse; so that most of them said, "He is dead." But Jesus took him by the hand and lifted him up, and he arose.

— Mk 9:25-27

FAITH AT WORK

Jesus had given his disciples the command and the power to cast out demons, and yet they could not cast this spirit out. Why did they fail? They wondered the same thing. His answer to them was, "This kind cannot be driven out by anything but prayer and fasting" (Mk 9: 28-29).

The first thing to note is that Jesus said, "This kind." The spirit at work in the boy may have been a stronger, more powerful spirit than the disciples had encountered, or one that was more deeply entrenched in the boy's identity and personality. Second, Jesus' response is a clear call to prayer and fasting. Based on these Scriptures, prayer and fasting has become a basic element in spiritual warfare.

Was Jesus telling the disciples that they should have prayed and fasted right there before trying to cast out the demon, or was he saying that they needed to be more given to a lifestyle of prayer and fasting? Remember, the disciples had been criticized for not fasting (Mt 9:14) and in the one example we have of their extended time of prayer (Gethsemane), they fell asleep. Was it greater power they needed — or was it greater sensitivity to the Holy Spirit, who could lead them to look at the bigger picture and enable them to calmly talk to a father in the midst of a demonic encounter? It is important to note that Jesus did not stop to pray and fast. He already had the authority that would come to his disciples in greater measure though a life of prayer and fasting.

Through fasting, we say no to self-reliance and yes to God. We feed our faith, rather than feeding our flesh. In John 4:34, after Jesus' encounter with the Samaritan woman at the well, he said, "Doing the will of him who sent me and bringing his work to completion is my food." St. Catherine of Siena often said that obedience to God "fattens our souls." If the Father calls us to fast as a normal part of life, then our obedience "fattens" our soul, making it more responsive to the Holy Spirit. While we fast, our physical hunger is a constant reminder of our spiritual hunger for the salvation and freedom of souls. It also constantly reminds us that it is not by bread alone that we live, but rather by every word that comes from the mouth of God (see Mt 4:4). Through prayer, we deepen our relationship with the Lord and our total dependence on him, which increases our sensitivity to the Holy Spirit. A life characterized by prayer and fasting is a life characterized by sacrifice. When we intercede in a sacrificial way for someone who is afflicted, we engage in an act of love that unites us with the heart of God for the one in need.

The gospel of Matthew records a third reason that Jesus gave the disciples for their lack of success. When the disciples came to Jesus privately and said, "Why could we not cast it out?" he said to them:

> "Because of your little faith. For truly, I say to you, if you have faith as a grain of mustard seed, you will say to this mountain, 'Move from here to there,' and it will move; and nothing will be impossible to you."
>
> — Mt 17:19-20

Taking these passages together, we see the connection between faith, prayer, and fasting. Prayer and fasting remove the hindrances to faith and enable us to experience the union we have with Christ. It is through faith in Christ that the captives are set free. Jesus modeled for his disciples a life of prayer and fasting, while walking in union with his Father: doing only what the Father was doing and following the lead of the Holy Spirit. Jesus did not give a formula for deliverance as much as an invitation to join him by faith.

Faith is a gift from God, by which we accept and respond to the full revelation of the mystery of Christ. By faith, we can tell a mountain to move and it will move. By faith, we believe that nothing is impossible for us who believe. Faith increases as we live our life for God, and as we remember his faithfulness, his answered prayers, and our personal breakthroughs. Faith increases when we yield to the truth of what God has said, what he has done, and who he has revealed himself to be. The father in this story spoke for us all when he said, "I believe, help my unbelief." When Jesus set the son free, he made a promise to us as well: "Nothing will be impossible to you" who take the smallest amount of faith and act on it.

A MAN IN NEED

In the New Testament, all recorded deliverance took place outside of Jerusalem, the center of Jewish worship. The region of the Gerasenes, where we find the most severe case of demonic possession,[32] was not only far from the center of faith, but also in the Decapolis, a place where Greek, Roman, and Jewish cultures converged. There, Jews — especially religious Jews — would have been a minority. Pagan temples, where every manner of sexual immorality predominated, dotted the countryside. Many scholars see Jesus' visit to the Decapolis as a prophetic act, anticipating the Church's mission to the Gentiles, for this trip was one of the rare occasions when he went to Gentile territory.

Jesus, on a mission from his Father, told his disciples to get into the boat and go to the area of Gerasa on the other side of the lake. Was he being sent because somebody had prayed for the demoniac and the Father was sending his Son to him? Or had this man heard about Jesus and, in a sane moment, cried out for help? We do not know, but we do know this trip was a very decisive action and that Jesus' primary accomplishment was setting the demoniac free.

The kingdom of darkness had a strong hold on the people of the Decapolis, and this poor man from Gerasa was in severe bondage. Even by modern standards, we would say that he was clearly possessed. Demons spoke though him; he was tormented so much that he cut himself; he had super-human strength; he lived without clothes in the tombs; he cried out day and night. This man's need for an exorcism seems obvious. An interview, so helpful for a non-confrontational style of deliverance, would no doubt not have worked in this situation.

This is the one passage in the New Testament where it appears that Jesus used an element of Jewish exorcism. After his command for the spirit to leave was met with shouting ("What do you want with me? . . . I beg you, don't torment me"), he responded with the question, "What is your name?" Discovering the name of the demon, or forcing it to reveal its name, gave the exorcist authority over it.

A name speaks to one's identity and the power to name expresses authority. We see this in Genesis when Adam named the animals, signifying his authority over them. If a demon hides its name, it can hide its identity and is free to work in the cover of darkness. So, when the demons responded to Jesus' question with the name "Legion," they may have been trying to avoid disclosure.

As we read the story in Luke 8, it appears that Jesus cast spirits out of this man through means that are similar to official exorcism, or at least a confrontational style of deliverance. Indeed, if the Gerasene demoniac were here today, I have no doubt the Church would consider him a candidate for exorcism. But we can also see revealed in this account important guidelines for the ministry of deliverance. Our study of this account can help us evaluate our current practice and shed light on the process that individuals go though as they receive an exorcism.

Uncovering the Legal Right

With an eye toward discovering these guidelines, let us look again at the story of the Gerasene demoniac (Lk 8:22-38.)

When Jesus suggested to his disciples that they go to the other side of the lake, he didn't tell them why. On the way over, a very unusual thing happened: Jesus fell asleep while a terrifying storm came down on the lake. I wonder if there wasn't something in the wind and waves that frightened the disciples more than a usual storm. They woke the Master, and he rebuked the wind and waves. Were these simply the forces of nature he rebuked, or was something else opposing their journey — something that Jesus would not have acknowledged, save for the terror of the disciples?

Jesus slept because he was at rest even in a storm of demonic proportion. His sleeping was also an opportunity for the disciples to grow and exercise their faith. This trip was part of their training, but they did not grasp that they were on a mission ordained by God. They looked at the natural; their spiritual eyes did not see demonic forces at work. Was Jesus teaching them to open their hearts to the spiritual nature of their mission when he asked, "Where is your faith?" When Jesus calmed the storm, they were left in awe of Jesus and afraid of him.

That is exactly how we should approach praying for someone for liberation. We should be in such awe of Jesus and his power that we no longer consider the distractions of the enemy. We need to learn to sleep through the spiritual opposition that keeps us from the purposes of God.

When Jesus arrived, the man possessed by demons came to meet him, revealing that he was not completely possessed. There was something in this man crying out for help, and God had heard him. His will was compromised, his true identity was being robbed from him and submerged under the demonic spirit, but he came to Jesus.

Jesus will not violate anyone's free will. If there were no part of this man asking for help, wanting to be free, then Jesus would not and, in fact, could not drive the demons out. He will always abide by the laws God established for fallen humanity. But this man came toward Jesus, signaling that there was a part of him that wanted to be free. Yet the man so identified with, and was so united to, the spirits within him that the presence of Jesus tormented him. It is not unusual for someone in this state to feel a burning at the mere touch of the hand by the one trying to help him or her. The presence of Jesus harasses the demon but the person feels the harassment as well. It is unlikely the man would be able to distinguish the difference between the demon's pain and his own.[33] Jesus provoked this torment and fear because he had commanded the spirit to come out.

Now, how is it that the Son of God can give a command to a demon and the demon not obey right away? Even though the command tortured the demons, they still did not release the man. He should have been set free like all the others to whom Jesus ministered. Was there another area of agreement with darkness that gave the demons a legal right to remain?

Demons have power through the action of men. Pagan worship, immorality, and deceitful practices bring the influence of evil spirits into the lives of individuals, local groups, or even nations. Such involvements with the kingdom of Darkness strengthens the devil's power in regions that God gave humans the authority to rule. He did not give ruling authority to angels or demons. But man, through sin and rebellion, yielded his authority to the enemy, increasing his influence not just in the heart of a person but also in the spiritual realm, which in turn can have influence over a region in the world.[34]

It seems that demons at work in the Gerasene demoniac had a legal right to be in that region. This right would have to have come through the actions and agreement of the people who lived there, either in the past or present. Pagan worship, a horrific act, injustice, or the like could establish a demon's claim in the region, a claim that could be broken only by the people who lived in that region. So even though the demons were tormented by the presence and command of Jesus, they stood on their legal rights. Even as they begged Jesus not to send them out of the region, they were bold — standing on their claim — so they did not immediately obey Jesus. They begged because they recognized the Son of God had absolute authority to do what he wished.

Revealing the True Identity

Did Jesus repeat his command or just speak it once? Scripture only reveals the one command. Not getting the proper response to the command, Jesus stopped and asked the man his name. Was Jesus asking for the man's name or was he asking for the name of the demon, as a Jewish exorcist would have done? Note that the Scripture says that Jesus *asked* for his name. Every other time Jesus addresses a demon with a command. Here, I believe, Jesus was directly addressing the troubled inner man. Jesus recognized the identity of the man, and thus asked him for his name. "Tell me your name; tell me who you are." He called out for the man whom God created, the man he still loved. In compassion, he called the true man to respond.

When the demons spoke, it was clear that they didn't want Jesus to connect with the man they held. The demons spoke a name that wouldn't reveal their identity, but rather described their strength: "I am Legion." The name Legion might intimidate some, but it was a laughable effort to attempt to intimidate the Son of God. The name Legion did not reveal the man's true identity, nor did it in any way reveal the legal right that the enemy had to this person, so it did not contribute to his release. Something had gone terribly wrong with this man. Whether he was abused, neglected, abandoned, or went without a sense of identity into a pagan temple, the demons had an open door into his life. Jesus could see that he needed, like all of us, to find his true name. Jesus did not use the name of Legion in the expulsion of the demons. He wants to reveal our true name, so that our true identity can be known.

After identifying themselves as Legion, the demons continued their torment and begged Jesus not to command them to depart into the abyss. The Gospel of Mark records that they begged to be sent into pigs instead of out of the region (see Mk 5:10-11). Now, another question arises. Why would Jesus give the demons permission to do anything destructive? I think that the primary reason was that Jesus would not violate the demons' legal right to be in the region. In addition, the destructive action of the demons was a visible warning to the people of the depth of their identification with darkness.

After the demons left, the townspeople saw this man in his right mind. They saw that the demons had gone from him, and they were afraid. No doubt, they were afraid of more than just the possibility of additional destruction. They may have been "seized with great fear," because a fear came upon them from another realm (see Lk 8:37) or because they experienced the sudden absence of the presence of the demonic to which they had become accustomed.

This Scripture brings two very important lessons to us. First, the enemy can only operate in our lives if he has a legal right to do so. If we have no desire to be free, or if we hold on to an area of unforgiveness, unrepented sin, or lies, then a demon will resist a command to leave, even if given in the name of Jesus. Repentance of sin, forgiveness of others and self, and renouncing the spirits and their attachments are necessary to break a demon's legal right to be in our lives. Agreement with the enemy's lies must be addressed and renounced in order to break his hold. We can then exercise the authority given to us by Jesus and take hold of the freedom we have been given in the Son of God by the Father.

Second, the purpose of deliverance is to enable us to answer the question, "What is your name?" Once the Kingdom has come in our lives, and the Lordship of God is experienced, our foundation needs to be restored. Redemption and healing must come to the damaged foundations. Although the former demoniac begged to go with Jesus after he had been healed, Jesus sent him home instead.

We all need to return home, in the sense that we need to face the things in the past that have bound us and allow the redemptive power of the cross to bring good out of evil, and victory out of defeat. In the process, we begin to realize that we have accepted false names. Did someone once tell you that you were worthless? Or a failure? Or even stupid? Those false names will be wiped out as we stand under the gaze of our Heavenly Father, who has always been our true home, and find our true identity as children of God. The new name we have been given in Christ — the name "Well-loved Son" or "Chosen Daughter" — will conquer all the false names we have carried throughout our lives.

The question for you today is, "What is your name?" When you speak your name, to whose voice do you give expression? Do you speak from your wounds, your self-doubt, or your hurt, anger, and resentment? Or do you speak from the knowledge that you are a beloved son or daughter of the Eternal Father? If Jesus, the Son of God, dwells in you and has redeemed you by your acceptance of His work on the cross, no matter what negative thing has attached itself to your self-understanding, you have been made a new creation, and have been given a new identity in Christ. As the newly whole man was sent home, we, too, must go home. We do this by taking our new identity in Christ to the place where our identity was first formed, into our early family dynamics and circumstances. We do this by turning our backs on distortions we have embraced and on lies we have so long accepted. We go home by believing that God has given us a gift in our human families and by setting our minds to discovering that gift.

CHAPTER 6

Encountering the Truth

Rather, we have renounced secret and shameful ways; we do not use deception, nor do we distort the word of God. On the contrary, by setting forth the truth plainly we commend ourselves to every man's conscience in the sight of God.

— 2 Cor 4:2

And you shall know the truth, and the truth shall set you free.

— Jn 8:32

When Jesus set the Gerasene demoniac free, he also called him home to his true identity. The complete change in life experienced by that newly restored man is the same change being experienced by Catholics today as they are delivered of the evil in which they have misplaced their true selves.

For example, Mary Anne had so lost her real self that, as she herself recently said, "Mary Anne was dead — she had no rights anymore." Note that Mary Anne talks about herself in the third person. She says that as the years passed, "Mary Anne remained dead; eventually, I forgot about her. I learned to be someone else. I became a superficial person. I gave up all my personal thinking, my personal opinions, and my personal ideas — I learned to take on the minds of those around me." How did Mary Anne misplace her true identity? By what process and understanding was she able to recover the person God had made her to be? Listen to her story, for it is instructive.

Mary Anne's Story

All my life I felt less than others, not good enough and rejected. Very shy, I wanted to make myself small so no one would notice me. I knew it bothered my parents, as I would hear Mom say to others, "Mary Anne is so shy. She won't talk." Hearing that, I felt even more rejected, so to compensate within, I would say quietly, "You want to see shy — I'll show you shyness." In my "felt" rejection, I was determined to be even shyer than before.

Whenever bad things happened to me, I felt I deserved them. I did not even tell my mom, for I had grown to believe that no one cared. I began to expect bad things to be my "lot" in life. It was easier to accept cruelty from someone than kindness. My childhood days, so many of which were spent alone, were filled with self-deprecation, self-hatred, and self-condemnation — all horrible things to live with. My only place of happiness was my imagination. This was my familiar pattern as I was growing up and it stuck with me. My biggest coping mechanism, to protect myself, was to let myself die. Inside I knew I had died; you see, no one could ever hurt me or reject me if I was dead. As I lay dead on the inside, I also determined to always agree with those around me. I became submissive and passive, because I thought that then I would belong, I would be part of "the group." It seemed to work, yet there I was, stuck on the outside looking in, never feeling a part of anything, never feeling worthy enough to really belong. I was in isolation, but didn't know it. My defensive walls were so thick and so strong that no one could get through. But I thought I was safe.

During my twenties, a dark period of my life, I believed I actually belonged to Satan. I believed I was going to hell and there was absolutely nothing I could do about it. Now I see that I chose to remain in bondage, but I was not aware of it at the time. I didn't pray, I didn't read scripture. Rarely did I take advantage of the great Sacrament of Reconciliation. I went to Mass, but didn't actively participate. I had given up. I was so sure that God couldn't and didn't love me. With all the people to love, surely he didn't have time for me. Though these thoughts were lies, I believed them. I was following Satan's plan for my life. In the choice between two kingdoms, I had unconsciously chosen the loser's kingdom.

Mary Anne may have chosen the "loser's kingdom," but God was not about to let her go. Over the years, he gently drew her, giving her an interest in reading the Bible, in praying the Scriptures, in listening for the Lord's voice, and in moving closer to Jesus. Yet something blocked her ability to get closer to the Lord. What was it? She began to struggle, asking for a breakthrough, yet fearing it all the same. She continued:

I knew there was an area in my life I didn't want to go to. It was heavy, dark, empty, and unwelcoming. I avoided it, for it was too frightening to go there. But in 2007, I read *Unbound* and went to the Freedom in Christ conference. There, I learned to ask for forgiveness, forgive others, and recognize the evil influences and lies that held me in bondage. As I renounced everything that held me, I could see that I was clearing the path to the one deep, dark, black, empty room within that I had a fear of entering. You know those old, wooden boards that read "KEEP OUT AND THAT MEANS YOU," that kids hang on the outside of their private clubhouses? That old crooked sign hung strong and heavy over my heart. But now I felt equipped with the tools I needed. Hope was on the horizon.

Over the next year, as Mary Anne grew in her faith, her awareness of this locked area began to increase. Finally, worn down by the struggle of avoiding that room, she called out to

God, who showed her what was inside — and turned on the light for her.

> God reminded me of a sense of heavy, thick darkness that had been in the back of my mind for many years. He gave me a picture of my mother, sad and crying while holding me or rocking me or walking with me. Somehow, I knew she was unhappy and desperate. Somehow, I knew this was my fear. It didn't make sense to me, but encouraged now by the things I experienced at the Unbound conference, I dared to allow the Holy Spirit to open that dreaded door. I knew I wanted total freedom.
>
> I was the fifth child to my parents. The oldest was only five by the time I was born; the brother immediately above me was six months old when I was conceived. My parents were very, very poor. Another child? You can imagine how they felt at that time. I believe this is what I felt in the womb — the darkness, the crying, the sadness, were signs of rejection. I was not wanted. For over sixty years I had believed and lived this rejection. Because of this lie, I had decided not to accept anything positive said to me, and always thought, "Yeah, right. They don't mean it. Don't believe them, there's an ulterior motive. Watch out! Don't trust!" if kindness and affirmation came my way.
>
> Fortunately, the Lord gave me a trustworthy friend who prayed with me and led me through the five keys again. Today, as I return to that formerly dark memory, I sense that I am a tiny speck completely engulfed in an indescribable Light. The awareness of love is greater than the sense of rejection had ever been before, and I sense the Lord saying, "See, I have loved you all the time. I wanted you. And I have always been with you from the very beginning." When that voice — such a disgusting, evil voice — says, "Right, yeah, right," I recognize that

it is not my voice, but the voice of my lying enemy. Immediately, I command it to leave in the name of Jesus.

I am free. I even walk differently now — as if I am not held down by gravity. Do I believe and feel that I am a beloved daughter of God? *You bet I do!* Do I know and feel His love for me? *You bet I do!* Do I let that rejection and those lies come back and take control? *NO!* Now I recognize it when it rears its ugly head. I know it; I face it and I rebuke it with the authority given me by Jesus Christ with the power of His Holy Name and it's gone. It has lost its power to lie to me anymore. I am free to be me. Mary Anne has been resurrected!

This story, like hundreds of others I have heard, is perhaps the most compelling reason why deliverance and exorcism need to be properly understood in the life of the Church. Recall Jesus' intense compassion when he responded:

> "And ought not this woman, a daughter of Abraham *whom Satan bound for eighteen years,* be loosed from this bond on the Sabbath day?"
> — Lk 13:16 (emphasis added)

How much more desperate are those who, like Mary Anne, have suffered for decades before finding real help!

Pope Paul the VI declared that evangelization is the essential mission of the Church,[35] and Mary Anne's story reveals what is at the heart of evangelization — the Good News, the liberating power of Jesus, is not just being presented to an unbelieving world but also into the darkness that binds believers from within. It is the ministry of Jesus to set the captives free, to destroy the works of the devil. This is the ministry of the Church that each of us needs to learn to participate in. This is the message we carry to a world bound by the works of darkness.

When I asked Mary Anne if I could use her story, she replied, "Of course, and I don't mind my name being used. I am so happy to have this freedom in Christ I want to shout out to everyone to get on board!" I believe this is God's heart as well. He wants to shout out. Is this not what Jesus said in John 7:37?

> On the last day of the feast, the great day, Jesus stood up and proclaimed, "If any one thirsts, let him come to me and drink."

For Mary Anne's voice to be heard, and for Mary Anne's freedom to be repeated throughout Christendom, both the deep need in the Church and the solution offered by God must be boldly revealed. The Church must overcome opposition, obstacles, misunderstandings, and the fear of the repetition of past abuse.

Our Great Need

A German radio documentary reported that hundreds of Germans, "tortured by inner voices, are looking for priests to help free them from what they believe to be the grip of the devil."[36] According to an article in the *Times Online*, Fr. Jeorg Mueller claimed to have received requests from some 350 people who thought they were possessed by an evil spirit. Mueller, who heads a group of priests, doctors, and therapists to deal with the problem, said, "Therapy hasn't worked for them; they want exorcism — a prayer that can free them."

Meanwhile, a CBN news article stated that in historically Catholic Italy, there are an estimated 800 Satanic cults operating in the country, with more than 600,000 followers. And according to Silvano Lilli, an evangelical pastor in Rome, their numbers are growing. "The devil's diabolical influence is growing in so many areas of our society," says Lilli. "He needs to be driven out."[37]

I have had the privilege of working with Catholics dedicated to evangelization in many countries. In one former Communist country, we discovered that almost 80 percent of the people we prayed with had at some time consulted an occult practitioner. In a church decimated by Communism, the people sought to fill their spiritual vacuum from sources apart from the Lord and his Church. Meanwhile, in several African countries we visited, we found that a majority of the Catholics we worked with had consulted with witchdoctors, seeking blessing, protection, or healing. Many Catholics had been taken by their own parents to these witchdoctors when they were quite young.

Catholics in the United States have a lot in common with Catholics in Europe and Africa. We may think of ourselves as "enlightened," but popular TV shows like *The Medium* and *Ghost Hunters* reveal the same trends. Rising interest in witchcraft and psychic hotlines, as well as in horoscopes and the paranormal, still lead people down a road to spiritual bondage. In referring to the occult, the Catholic *Catechism* is clear:

> All forms of divination are to be rejected: recourse to Satan or demons, conjuring up the dead or other practices falsely supposed to "unveil" the future. Consulting horoscopes, astrology, palm reading, interpretation of omens and lots, the phenomena of clairvoyance, and recourse to mediums all conceal a desire for power over time, history, and, in the last analysis, other human beings, as well as a wish to conciliate hidden powers. They contradict the honor, respect, and loving fear that we owe to God alone. (2116)

> All practices of magic or sorcery, by which one attempts to tame occult powers, so as to place them at one's service and have a supernatural power over others — even if this were for the sake of restoring their health — are gravely contrary to the virtue of religion. (2117)

Yet when was the last time you heard the clarion warning from the pulpit?

If Mary Anne could completely lose her selfhood just from the internal vows she had made as a child, how much more bondage will a Catholic enter when he dabbles in the occult? Does your story include the magical and mysteriously supernatural? Does your story sound more like Mary Anne's? Is there someone you know who has a hidden story of torment that needs to be heard and brought under the power of the One who died to save her? Though unaware, the world is crying out for the freeing grace God has bestowed upon the Church.

IS THE CHURCH PREPARED?

No, we are not. Fr. Gabriel Amorth, the chief exorcist of Rome, has said, "Even within the Church, we have a clergy and an episcopate who no longer believe in the devil, in exorcisms, in the extraordinary evil that the devil can cause, nor in the power that Jesus has given us to drive out demons."[38] He went on:

> For three centuries, the Latin Church — in contrast with the Orthodox Church and various Protestant confessions — has *almost entirely abandoned the ministry of exorcism* [emphasis added]. As the clergy no longer practice exorcisms, as they no longer study them and have never seen them, they no longer believe in them. And nor do they believe in the devil either. We have entire episcopates that are hostile to exorcisms.

Both statistical and anecdotal evidence suggests that Catholics in developing countries are leaving the Church for Pentecostalism in large numbers. The Ugandan bishop with whom we worked confirmed this trend in his own country. When he asked us to teach his priests about deliverance ministry, he said that many of his people were leaving the Catholic Church and joining Pentecostal churches in order to find help in breaking free of demonic bondages.[39]

The need is no less great in North America. I receive calls and e-mails regularly from Catholics who believe they need deliverance ministry, and I don't know where to send them. Why is the power of Christ not being brought to the needy through a simple expression of the Gospel like the five keys of Unbound? Why do some dioceses not provide exorcism for the extreme cases?

Opposition Arising from Confusion

As I began to write my first book on deliverance, I asked a priest active in the deliverance ministry for his advice. His response? "It would have been better if you had written it ten years ago." This priest told me of a rumor, widely disseminated in the Church, which held that only a priest could use the imperative — a command for a spirit to leave. That would mean that a lay person using non-confrontational deliverance could not exercise his or her authority to dismiss a demon that lurked behind debilitating lies. Although this was a rumor, the priest believed that the Church was moving in this direction, if it had not made the prohibition already. I listened to the priest with dismay. A part of me was discouraged, thinking, "I guess I'm too late."

Fortunately, another part of me became more passionate to write about what I had been learning. I believed that what the Lord has imparted to me would address many of the pastoral concerns of bishops and pastors. Knowing that if the Holy Spirit had given me some wisdom in deliverance, it could not be in disagreement with the Church's teaching, I set out to find the source and the veracity of the rumor. I knew that I might be wrong, but I hoped to find the rumor unsubstantiated. And indeed, I discovered that though the idea that the imperative command was reserved for priests had become common among Catholics at many levels, it had not been officially taught by the Church. I also found the theological basis for it to be very weak.

The *Catechism* identifies exorcism itself with the public ministry of the Church.

> When the Church asks *publicly* [emphasis added]
> and authoritatively in the name of Jesus Christ that a
> person or object be protected against the power of
> the Evil One and withdrawn from his dominion, it is
> called exorcism.
>
> — CCC 1673

Those who have made a case for restricting the word of command to the priest have failed to make a distinction between public ministry of exorcism and the private ministry, which is called deliverance. In his doctoral dissertation in canon law, Fr. Jeffrey S. Grob wrote:

> An exorcism is considered "public" when an authorized
> person using an approved rite does it in the name of the
> Church. A "private" exorcism is not bound by the same
> constraints and may be celebrated by any of the faithful.[40]

It is likely that a misunderstanding of the distinction between public and private exorcism arose for the same reason the Church placed boundaries around exorcism through the centuries: the Church is responding to abuses. For surely, there have been abuses of the use of this charism.

I know of people who have been hurt though confrontational deliverance and exorcisms. Some people have been hurt because no freedom has come, although they entrusted themselves, in vulnerability and hopefulness, to someone who did not help. Some have been hurt because insensitive people have blamed them for abandoning the spiritual battle. Others have been hurt by judgments and accusations spoken in the context of a confrontational deliverance or exorcism. I have spoken to men and women who have been hurt and humiliated when the minister actually sat on them, yelled at them, or poured oil down their throats in an attempt to torment and drive the demons away.

Such abuses horrify us. However, it is important not to draw erroneous conclusions about the result of these abuses. Recently,

Fr. Francis Martin announced that his friend Fr. Rufus Pereira had asked then-Cardinal Ratzinger whether only a priest could command a spirit to leave a person. The Cardinal's answer: the restriction was not intended for private ministry.[41] This is in keeping with past tradition. Fr. James McManus, CSsR, wrote:

> St. Alphonsus stated the Catholic tradition when he said that *everyone may exorcise privately*, but only the priest, with the permission of the bishop, may exorcise solemnly.[42]

Thus, although the controversy has swirled in the highest circles, we can be assured that deliverance ministry is an open path to spiritual freedom for Catholics.[43]

Opposition Arising from Unbelief

Many Catholics have abandoned the belief in the devil and regard evil spirits as "medieval." They act as though we now have a superior knowledge of human personhood that eliminates the need to address the influence of evil in any way, except through repentance of sin and confession. Ironically, though, we cannot properly understand sin if we do not believe in the devil. And we cannot gain access to the power of the Gospel by adopting a worldview that excludes spiritual forces that influence the human person. Pope John Paul II made it very simple: "If you do not believe in the devil, you do not believe in the Gospel."[44]

Opposition Arising from Fear

Many others live in fear, acting as if Satan had as much power as God, even though official Church teaching has long rejected this dualistic heresy (*CCC* 285).

When I was in Africa, one of the problems I found was that many Catholics believed evil spirits flew around, landing on people indiscriminately. They thought that a spirit could be sent by a spoken curse or could simply decide to attack a person.

Curses are real, but the actual doorway to the affliction of evil spirits is opened through superstition, ignorance of truth, and fear. Because many Catholics were under superstition and fear, their priests dismissed their experience of demonic attack.

The same fears exist among Catholics in the Unites States as well. Men and women who are afflicted by demons are often led down an over-spiritualized path. They may be enamored with the mystery of evil. They may believe that they are afflicted for no reason except God's mysterious purposes. No doubt there is a level of mystery to any torment, but to make this mystery the result of noble purpose often leaves the victim helpless and powerless. One woman told me that she was suffering demonic attack as a result of the spiritual consequences of her aunt's abortion. This interpretation took all the focus off of her life and her own responsibility. It kept her from accepting that God wanted to help her with her own role as a wife and mother.

Sometimes fear is compounded when an unhealthy belief in the devil's power joins with over-attentiveness to rumors. When one man I know promoted the *Unbound: Freedom in Christ* conference among his acquaintances, he was given a one-page declaration of warning that included the following:

> Every direct command and only a direct command to the devil is properly called an exorcism…Anyone performing any imprecatory exorcism without authorization is in extreme danger. I can't emphasize this more. If one plays with fire, one WILL GET BURNT!

A Catholic who is not clear about the all-surpassing power of Jesus Christ is more susceptible to the strength of rumors and the influence of those who attempt to control others through such dire warnings.

Fear of the process itself also leads to opposition within the clergy and may keep a Catholic from seeking the deliverance he needs. The seeker may mistakenly believe that he will be forced to experience the sometimes violent and certainly embarrassing manifestation of the demon as it leaves. The priest may not have any applicable training and may not want to deal with a manifestation. Both depend on the false assumption that the driving away of evil spirits must be accompanied by manifestations. But in my experience, what we expect in the area of demonic manifestations is what we get. If we expect wild behavior, or demonic distortions of the human body, we will probably get them.

This is one reason that I'm concerned when some people are incorrectly labeled as "possessed" if there is a manifestation. We need to keep in mind that some manifestations are not demonic at all, but deep emotional wounds and pain being released by the presence of God. Other manifestations are generated by cultural beliefs and expectations associated with deliverance or exorcism. These factors do not discount the real, unavoidable manifestations that occur in those that are severely demonized or possessed.

Many exorcists and some in the deliverance ministry begin by confronting demons — which provokes manifestations. This is how God has led some to help others gain freedom. It may be their charism; I thank God for those who serve in this way. But because of the potential for increased fear, confrontation may not be the best place to start when helping bring someone to freedom.

Using the Unbound Model, I rarely see manifestations. This is primarily because I do not expect manifestations, nor do I minister to a person in a way that leads him to expect manifestations. Since my focus is on the individual, I do not confront spirits. Instead, I help him close the doors that have been opened to his enemy. Once the person, as a child of God with authority, renounces his enemies and takes his stand against the devil's schemes (Eph 6), I simply command in the name of Jesus that the evil spirits leave.

Those who come to us for ministry follow our lead. If manifestations do occur, I see them first as a teaching opportunity. With the proper encouragement, the believer learns that he can take control over manifestations and discovers in the process that he has authority over the enemy. Second, I see manifestations as a sign that God is working to bring to the surface things that have been hidden rather than a sign that demons need to be confronted. The Unbound Model, as you can see, is a non-confrontational approach that Catholics can safely practice without fear.

OVERCOMING FEAR

Of course, if you believe evil spirits are afflicting you, you should go to your pastor or to someone you are confident you can trust. If they believe evil spirits are affecting you, don't be surprised if you run into fear. It may not be your own fear but the fear of others. Lay people may say you need a priest; the priest may say you need a holy priest; the holy priest may be too humble and say you need a charismatic priest or an exorcist appointed by the bishop. Others will only point to the traditional means of grace, prayer, fasting, and sacraments, or they may add a psychiatrist to the suggestions. Some of these responses arise from unbelief or ignorance, but many of them come from fear.

One of Pope John Paul II's central messages, proclaimed throughout his Papacy, was "Do not be afraid." Sometimes, well-meaning Catholics reinterpret fear as prudence or as the cautiousness that comes from wisdom. It is essential to understand our own (and others') motives realistically, honestly, "in the light." Sacred Scripture proclaims, "Perfect love casts out fear" (1 Jn 4:18). When we "walk" in our identity as beloved children of an all-powerful Father, we have nothing to fear. Recently, Pope Benedict spoke about how true liberation is experienced in Christ, who gives us victory over fear of spirits.

For the pagan world, which believed in a world full of spirits, mostly dangerous and against which one had to defend oneself, the proclamation that Christ is the only victor and that he who is united to Christ did not have to fear anyone, appeared as a true liberation. To these people (he refers to paganism of today), it is necessary to announce that Christ is the conqueror, such that one who is with Christ, who remains united to him, should not fear anything or anyone. It seems to me that this is also important for us, who should learn to face all fears, because he is above every domination, he is the true Lord of the world.[45]

Fear of the devil, you see, is based on deception, not on the truth. It is based on the lie that Jesus cannot stand up to the devil, that God is not strong enough to protect us. And yet, 2 Peter 1:3 tells the follower of Christ, "His divine power has granted to us all things that pertain to life and godliness." It is clear that the devil has no power when confronted with the power of Christ. Paul reminds us of how much power we have:

The weapons of our warefare are not worldly but have divine power to destroy strongholds.

— 2 Cor 10:4

Mary Anne experienced that divine power. The stronghold that had taken her very identity captive was demolished by the truth of the love of Christ. She received her self back again.

There are so many Mary Annes who are in bondage of one sort or another. We cannot let fear, misunderstandings, or complacency keep us from hearing the voice of Mary Anne, and the multitudes like her, who want to encounter the Truth that sets the captive free.

CHAPTER 7

Deliverance Ministry — A Pastor's Insight

And Jesus asked him, "What is your name?" He replied,
"My name is Legion; for we are many."

— Mk 5:9

Pope Benedict has boldly proclaimed, "If we are united to Christ, we should fear no enemy and no adversity." The purpose of deliverance ministry is to remove every obstacle to this union with Christ. The purpose of deliverance is to remove the fears and the lies that you have embraced, keeping you from trusting in the truth that Christ indeed is Lord of the universe and Lord of your life.

Ignorance of truth is one source of fear. Evil spirits present themselves as more powerful than they really are ("My name is Legion"), as if they can resist the Lord himself. It may be true that a person has submitted to the enemy's influence and become bound beyond his ability to resist, but we do not resist the enemy in our own name or simply by our willpower; we resist in the name and authority of Jesus.

Learning that there is a fine line between the work of an evil spirit and a particular lie, sin, or trauma has been very helpful to me. In deliverance ministry, identifying the spirit may not even be necessary as long as the particular bondage or "negative force" behind which the spirit is hiding is identified. Fr. James Wheeler, S.J., describes five types of bondage by which a human being is trapped, moving from the most basic forms of demonic oppression to the most serious. The levels of bondage identified by Fr. Wheeler are negative emotions, bondage from possessive relationships, harassment from outside spirits, obsession or oppression, and possession.[46] These are practical observations made by a man steeped in the wisdom of St. Ignatius of Loyola, combined with his years of experience in full-time healing ministry. I find his categories very helpful for practical understanding.

A Negative Force — the Basic Level of Influence

Christians often experience negative emotions such as guilt, resentment, or jealousy. Wheeler recognizes that evil spirits work within the heart to exaggerate the negative emotion that is present as a result of "a long standing pattern of sin or self-negation that is often unconscious to the person that needs to be released."[47] For example, he explains that when he says, "In the name of Jesus, we command the spirit of resentment to leave," the person will often testify that the emotional bondage to which they were subject "was broken at that moment."[48] He goes on:

> Indeed, the evil spirit, as St. Ignatius warns us in the rules for discernment of spirits, may exaggerate the fear, the anger, the guilt or whatever happens to be the particular weakness of the person. In such a case, to rebuke and take a strong stand against the power that seems to overwhelm might be in order.[49]

I have found that most people, at some point in their lives, benefit from this type of deliverance, which addresses both negative areas of their personality that have developed over time and the spirits that inhabit these patterns.

Bondage from Possessive Relationships

We are created to thrive in relationships, but sometimes a relationship can be controlling in a way that harms us. Wheeler believes that demons can take advantage of such possessive relationships, whether the relationship is with another person still living or one long dead, to further our bondage. I have witnessed how deep this bondage can go. Immoral and possessive relationships, soul-ties with former sexual partners, claims that a family member involved in the occult placed upon the victim: these and other possessive bondages are empowered or inhabited by evil spirits.

HARASSMENT

Harassment from outside spirits can come through suggestions, thoughts, or exaggerations of what is already in the individual. The spirits prey upon the weakness of the person. Although ordinarily, we call this harassment simply "temptation," I prefer to call it "compulsive temptation," to distinguish it from the fleeting thoughts of sin that come to all. As Fr. Wheeler writes:

> What seems to be the opinion of the Fathers and of Ignatius is that the inflammation of weakness within the personality is often the work of the evil spirit. And so the exacerbation of these points of influences such as lust, hatred, bitterness, etc., refers to the action of the evil one who is exploiting these points to his own advantage.[50]

Many view the demonic activity of these first three categories as relatively mild. They suggest that in these areas, the word of command is not required. They may question whether spirits are actually involved at this level. Jesus did not hesitate to point to the fact that we are influenced by demons. He taught us to pray, asking the Father to "Deliver us from the evil one." One of the gifts of the Unbound non-confrontational approach is that we can break the power of whatever level of this lesser bondage we experience; we can stand on the truth and, in the name of Jesus, command our Enemy to leave.

OBSESSION AND POSSESSION

It would behoove any Catholic who recognizes his own struggles in Wheeler's first three paradigms to deal with his issues as soon as possible, since these first three categories described by Fr. Wheeler are the doorway to the greater bondage of obsession, his final category prior to possession. At the level of obsession, significant areas of a person's life are held in bondage. Wheeler carefully defines obsession (he includes oppression also) as a situation either where some person or evil has seized control of an area of the personality, causing an extreme affliction and deep temptation, or where several areas of the personality have been affected. This much demonic control over time can lead directly to possession, which, as Wheeler defines it, occurs when a force not identifiable as the person's own will has taken total control of the personality. How can we tell someone to wait until they are in serious bondage before they learn to give expression to the fact the God in Christ has given us victory over our enemies?

Of course, we cannot and should not. People all over the world are saying "Yes!" as they discover the authority they have been given, as sons and daughters of God, to stand against their enemies and take hold of spiritual freedom. I have already described the five keys of the Unbound Model as a practical approach to those who are experiencing bondage. Learning to recognize the ultimate deception underlying demonic activity will empower the Catholic believer to receive his baptismal inheritance — the freedom won for him at the cross.

FATHER OF LIES

The common thread among his first four levels of demonic influence is that each is fueled by a lie. Jesus tells us that Satan is the father of lies. All lies trace themselves back to the original lie, "God is not a good Father, and he cannot be trusted." This lie accompanies every sin. Every negative emotion within is born out of the lie. The evil one whispers this lie indirectly through original sin and the distortion in our thinking that comes with every sin — or directly, through the thoughts that he presents to our imaginations as we process life's experiences. One lie built upon another lie eventually yields a pattern of thinking. If our thinking patterns are built out of lies and deceptions, we have made a place for the enemy to dwell. Ephesians tells us to not allow the enemy to establish a dwelling.

> Be angry but do not sin; do not let the sun go down on your anger, and give no opportunity to the devil.
>
> — Eph 4:26-27

Spirits are present wherever they focus their attention. When we sin, they are drawn like flies. If they perceive our vulnerability to sin, they will focus on it. If we sin and do not repent quickly, they will present to us thoughts and images that ustify our sin, or that draw us into deeper agreement with our sin. The lies that are part of every sin find a place to be rooted within our hearts. As our thoughts agree with the enemies' lies, they become entangled and joined with the lies. To the degree that we have surrendered to a demon's lie, we have become entangled not just with a false thought but with the spirit behind it.[51]

Paul, warning us not to give the devil a foothold, shows us that the first line of attack is usually on the emotions. We are wounded and hurt by someone. Then the mind is open to the lie. If we make a home for the lie, we also make a place for the enemy. Then, we find that the lies affect our thoughts, our will, and our emotions because of un-repented or even unrecognized sin. Our thinking patterns are meant to be a dwelling of the Holy Spirit; if they are given over to the enemy instead, these demon-infested thoughts need to be exposed. As we are increasingly converted, we expose them to the light of God, naming the lies and renouncing them aloud.

The Israelites understood that the spoken word has power, that a word spoken aloud releases what it represents. God said "Let there be light," and light appeared. God's people named their children — and thereby released them to fulfill their destinies. They passed their blessings on to the next generation not through written wills, but through the word spoken aloud. A spoken blessing, as a word from God, imparts good; a spoken lie, because it is spiritual as well, removes good. As one who ministers to another, you can help a believer take hold of her freedom by teaching her to renounce either the lie or the spirit behind the lie. Teach the believer to say, "In the name of Jesus, I renounce the lie that I am worthless," or "In the name of Jesus, I renounce a spirit of worthlessness." Sometimes, when I give the command, I command every lie the person has renounced to leave. It matters not whether someone renounces the spirit or simply renounces the lie: the renunciation "in the name of Jesus," breaks the spirit's power just the same. The lie and the spirit came together, and they must leave together.

Any Catholic whose life responses fall into one of Wheeler's first four categories will benefit when they expose and renounce the lie. He must tell his story, expose the darkness in his heart to the light, and respond in the name of Jesus. When he does this, the believer will almost always enter into a new level of freedom. Let me give an example.

Joan is a gifted woman with remarkable intellectual abilities. She studied theology and later began working toward her doctorate in history. Yet, a year into her studies, she dropped out; in fifteen years, she did not go back to school, nor was she able to "land" into any field of work or study. She was, in fact, deeply depressed and filled with self-hatred. This self-loathing manifested in her relationships as a critical, judgmental spirit one day, and as self-pity the next. What approach should be taken to help Joan?

She had already tried counseling, spiritual direction, the sacraments, prayer, and even prayer for inner healing, all of which were helpful to a degree. In all her search for help, why was deliverance not considered? Was it because of misunderstandings and fear of abuse? Was it because, in ignorance, someone thought deliverance was more complicated than it is? Is it possible that the devil himself had a hand in keeping deliverance ministry away?

On the other hand, what if someone had become suspicious of the presence of an evil spirit, and considered confronting the demons in the name of Jesus until they manifested? This may have amounted to an unauthorized invasion of Joan's soul and opened up areas of her life that she was not ready to address. Attempting to identify the names of demons would not have been appropriate for Joan. We are dealing with the work of evil spirits, or the spiritual forces behind a person's bondage. For this reason, the specific ancient name of the demon is not of interest to us, nor do we want to provoke the demonic spirit. Rather, we are interested in the generic name or characteristic, which identifies what the demon does.

So, in Joan's case, her freedom came when she was able to identify the lie empowering the self-pity, the critical spirit, and the depression. Satan is the accuser, and for years had been accusing Joan of worthlessness, which came out of childhood rejection. Her mother, not nurtured herself, had been unable to nurture Joan. How Joan came to be in spiritual bondage was more important than the exact spirit behind that bondage. When we dealt with the cause, and when Joan forgave her mother and renounced rejection — and the lie that she was worthless — the spirit that had attached itself to her left. Joan reports that since that time, she is able to receive God's love and finally understands her place as God's beloved daughter. Just as important, she is no longer trapped by the involuntary reactions that hindered her relationships; now, her ongoing freedom has given her a newfound ability to actually hear what people say and respond to them in love.

In a case like Joan's, I am aware that it's very possible that I will be leading her to renounce some things that really don't connect with her deep heart issues. Yet there is no harm done, as long as she is not renouncing something good, such as a God-given emotion. If it is not perfectly clear, I will often say, "Much of what you are renouncing are just flies (after all, Scripture calls the devil Beelzebub — the Lord of the flies); you will know if something is bigger or deeper." Because I do not always know whether a spirit is operating or not, I command "any spirit that Joan has renounced" to leave. I allow each person to decide which enemies were defeated through the power of Christ. I am certain that the believer has just renounced lies and negative emotions that do not come from God. Helping her understand that there was an entryway, a door to evil that she can close, encourages the believer to deal with helplessness and fear. This is part of evangelization that needs to take place to equip Catholics to be spiritually awake and alert. St. Peter tells us:

> Be sober, be watchful. Your adversary the devil prowls around like a roaring lion, seeking some one to devour. Resist him, firm in your faith, knowing that the same experience of suffering is required of your brotherhood throughout the world.
>
> — 1 Pet 5:8-9

Again, this is the work of every member of the Church.

What would have happened if we had confronted the spirits in Joan without addressing the area of attachment that gave them the legal right to be present? Joan might have manifested a presence of a spirit binding her or a spirit that had a "foothold" in her.[52] The confrontation might have opened the portal to the demonic source of the bondage. Once Joan manifested the demon, her deliverance could have become more complicated, for she would have had the experience of yielding temporary control of her consciousness to a demon. She might have been frightened or embarrassed, and less willing to undergo such an experience again. In the aftermath, she might have found herself more vulnerable to demonic manifestations that would distract her from the lies she needs to recognize and renounce.

Fortunately, the need for direct confrontation of a demon or an official exorcism is rare. Most troubled Christians have a level of demonic activity in their lives that fits squarely within the parameters of Wheeler's first four types of bondage. In order to effectively help most Catholics, we do not need to have esoteric knowledge of angels and demons; we do not need to know if the individual is feeling the touch of a part of a demon's personality; we do not need to know the names of demons.[53] An official exorcist of the Church may need to know these things, but what the rest of us need to know is that relative to Jesus Christ, all evil — whether it is a seemingly ten-foot kickboxing demon or a midget demon — is insignificant. If the individual who has come to us for help is a believer, then Jesus has already bound the strongman and is ready to take back what was stolen. The Lord simply waits for the person's cooperation.

Very rarely, the Church will determine that a person is actually possessed. Great care must be taken in making such a determination, as much harm may result to the believer's self-image and his understanding of God and his love. A misdiagnosis may create more problems for someone who really needs healing for a psychological disorder. For the same reason, we should exercise this same care before dealing with demonic activity through a confrontational deliverance. Even though a manifestation of a demon may appear, a confrontational deliverance is not necessarily required. The priest or leader can learn how to take control of the situation by leading the individual through an interview and non-confrontational deliverance. Thus, we should not take the lead from the demonic manifestation. Fr. Wheeler writes:

> Direct confrontations with evil would not have allowed the process of love, repentance, and healing to grow to a point where real healing would take place.[54]

He also cautions against seeking information through dialogue with a spirit.

> I am basically not in favor of getting this information through any spirit that is in that person because I believe that this gives the evil spirits a temporary control over the person's consciousness that is frightening and may be detrimental to that person.[55]

As Wheeler implies, our first concern needs to be the individual. We should be very careful about allowing demons to manifest their presence, because the true context of deliverance ministry and exorcism must always be evangelization. Deliverance is part of the evangelization of every person. If a person has been raised Catholic but has never been personally evangelized, the minister of deliverance must introduce him to the power of the Gospel. Then, letting him discover for himself the reality of the influence of evil spirits can lead to a new level of Christian maturity. There is no need for the Catholic to fear deliverance; Jesus himself, who comes to us in love and gentleness, is the true Deliverer. "Come to me," Jesus said, "all who labor and are heavy-laden, and I will give you rest. Take my yoke upon you and learn from me; for I am gentle and lowly in heart, and you will find rest for your souls" (Mt 11:28-29).

The process of leading another Catholic into deliverance is remarkably simple. Abigail's story illustrates this well. I spent an hour listening to her story, and then I led Abigail to express repentance, forgiveness, and renunciation of her enemies. When she finished, I gave the command, "In the name of Jesus, I command any spirit that Abigail has renounced to leave right now."

"I felt this excruciating pain in my upper back when you said it," Abigail said.

"I want you to let that pain be a backdrop and not the focus. It probably is just a distraction from you seeing what you need to see." I was quiet for a moment. "What's coming to your mind?" I asked.

"I see a bowling alley and the pins are being lifted up."

"How many pins are left?"

"Two."

"Good. We are close."

The next moment, Abigail remembered someone she needed to forgive. As she shared, she said she remembered that she thought that this world was not a very good place to be. This was the lie; it was a thread that could be seen throughout her life, from her conception, to her youth prior to marriage, to her numerous surgeries and rejections, to her work in a children's hospital with the saddest cases of sickness and death. The Holy Spirit revealed the thread, Abigail's renunciation removed it, and together, they destroyed the lie in a quiet way.

"In the name of Jesus, I renounce the lie that this life is not a good place to be," she prayed.

"In the name of Jesus, I break the power of the lie and command it to leave."

It was done. There were no more pins left on the alley for her to deal with on that day.

Just as Jesus could only do what his Father did, so we can only do what the Father is doing. What is the Father doing in the Church today? He is leading every person to freedom in the Son, and the Son is leading us into the heart of the Father, where we find our true identity and our life's purpose.

CHAPTER 8

Deliverance and the Sacrament of Reconciliation

Entrusting myself to the power of Jesus' forgiveness, letting myself be led by the hand by him, I can get out of the quicksand of pride and sin, of lies and sadness, of selfishness and every false certainty, to know and live the richness of his love.

— Benedict XVI, Angelus, January 25, 2009

The Church's desire, like the Lord's desire, is that each of her people find true freedom in the Son, and learn to know the Father personally. The sacrament of Reconciliation releases the grace of forgiveness into our lives and draws us into reconciliation with God. When we are reconciled to God, to others, and to ourselves, we can know both our true identity and our life's purpose.

I am often asked how the Unbound Model of deliverance fits into parish life and how it relates to the sacrament of Reconciliation. Is it possible that the Unbound Model in some way takes away from the sacrament? Is it possible that people may use it as a substitute for the sacrament? These are good questions. As you will see, however, non-confrontational deliverance supports the sacrament.

We receive the benefits of the sacrament — grace, forgiveness, and reconciliation — by faith. God meets us, in the sacrament, at whatever level of faith is present within our hearts; he takes the faith we come with and imparts greater faith to us so that we can receive his love more deeply. As the Lord renews our minds, and as he continually draws us into conversion, we are able more and more to receive the power in the dynamic message of the Gospel.

This is what we mean by evangelization. Pope Benedict reminds us of the Gospel's power when he writes that the Gospel is:

> . . . a message endowed with plenary authority, a message that is not just talk, but reality. In the vocabulary of contemporary linguistic theory, we would say that the *evangelium*, the Gospel, is not just informative speech, but performative speech—not just the imparting of information, but action, efficacious power that enters into the world to save and transform.[56]

The Gospel proclaimed and worked out in our life prepares us for all the sacraments. Deliverance is practical evangelization.

The liberation gained through deliverance is normally followed by an increased appreciation for the importance of the sacrament of Reconciliation. The Unbound Model, you may remember, is neither a prescribed method nor a magic formula for inner healing. Instead, it uses the universal aspects of the Gospel, the same Gospel that is proclaimed through the sacrament. As such, it is easily used by those with spiritual responsibility to complement the sacrament.

A priest who heard the confessions during a week's conference on the Unbound Model said that the confessions were "terrifyingly honest." Another priest told a penitent who came to him following one of our conferences, "This is the most honest confession you have ever made." Unbound teaches that the keys to take hold of our freedom in Christ are repentance and faith, forgiveness, renunciation, authority, and the Father's blessing. Scripture and Tradition present each of these keys as important aspects of the normal Christian life of faith; the sacraments also present these keys, in one form or another, to the believer. Let us consider, then, how the Unbound Model of deliverance fits into parish life and how it can support the sacrament of Reconciliation.

Your Catholic Heritage

Deliverance ministry is never intended to be seen apart from normal Catholic life. Deliverance is part of ongoing conversion. After our teaching one week, one priest told us that he added renunciation to his daily prayer. He inserted it right after his daily examination of conscience and seeking the Lord's pardon. The principles we teach, and that this priest embraced, are our heritage as Catholics. We have all been invited by the Father to encounter his love in Jesus Christ. We see this clearly in the sacrament of Reconciliation. There is no defect in the sacrament, yet many penitents fail to receive the grace offered.

For this reason, it is not enough to try to convince people of the sacrament's importance, nor simply to make it easier to receive. Rather, we must help people approach the sacrament in a way that is life-transforming. For it is through an encounter with the Lord in the sacrament that the life-transforming grace of the sacrament is released. Precisely because the priest is acting with the authority of Jesus Christ, the penitent is able to have a real encounter with Jesus. When people drink of the waters of life by encountering Jesus, they will come back for more.

But what of those who receive the grace of Reconciliation in a very limited way? Again, the sacrament is capable of conveying what it promises; the blockage to grace is within the person. As the *Catechism* teaches:

> The sacraments act *ex opere operato* . . . From the moment that a sacrament is celebrated in accordance with the intention of the Church, the power of Christ and his Spirit acts in and through it. . . . Nevertheless, the fruits of the sacraments also depend on the disposition of the one who receives them.
>
> — *CCC* 1128

If a person is to approach the sacrament with freedom and grace, he must embrace the power of the Gospel received in baptism. In our renewal of baptism, we learn to take our stand against the devil, to renounce his works and his empty promises, and to embrace the precepts of the faith.

RECONCILIATION AS A RENEWAL OF BAPTISM

Over the course of history, the Church has understood the sacrament of Reconciliation as a renewal of baptism. During the third and fourth centuries, Christians underwent extensive preparation for baptism. This preparation did not include detailed instruction about the mysteries of the sacraments, but focused instead on leaving the world, crucifying the flesh, and renouncing the devil. baptism was a death to the old life, an exit from the dominion of darkness and an entry into the Kingdom of God. In baptism, a man or woman became a new creation in Christ, entering into eternal life. Every personal conversion, every encounter with the Lord's truth and compassion, further released the transforming power of his baptism. Just so, the sacrament of Reconciliation brings to life this transformation in us. The sacrament confers the life-giving power of God.

However, if a penitent does not understand the Gospel of Jesus Christ, her approach to the sacrament of Reconciliation will hinder her reception of grace. For example, if a woman has never known unconditional acceptance, she may find her worth in being good or in doing the right thing. In this case, scrupulosity, perfectionism, or self-justification may motivate her confession. Unless these underlying issues are addressed, reception of the sacrament will not lift her burden. Instead of the joy of returning to the Lord and his love, confession may bring her only momentary relief. Her struggle to overcome a lifelong battle with unworthiness will continue shortly after leaving the confessional. Even worse, she may give up going to confessionat some point, because of a belief that she will never be good enough. She is unable to believe the Gospel message that God's unconditional, unchanging love for the world (Jn 3:16) includes her as well.

So, the challenge for the priest and minister is this: how do we help people approach the sacrament free from the lies that hold them bound, so they come able to name their sin and experience an encounter with the Lord that produces radical change?

UNBOUND AS A RENEWAL OF BAPTISM

The five keys of deliverance presented in the Unbound Model are also a renewal of baptism in the sense that the believer is making a personal decision to respond in faith to the revelation of the Savior, to forgive others, and to renounce the lies of the enemy. In doing so, he is following the command in Ephesians 6 to "stand."

> Put on the whole armor of God, that you may be able to stand against the wiles of the devil. . . . Therefore take the whole armor of God, that you may be able to withstand in the evil day, and having done all, to stand.
> — Eph 6:11, 13-14a

Having used the five keys of deliverance, the penitent is empowered. Rather than coming to confessionwith a helpless or "poor me" attitude, he comes as a member of the Church Militant who is fighting sin, deception, and all the works of the devil. He is ready to meet Jesus in the confession of sin, he is ready to be forgiven, and he is empowered to go forth into battle through the words of absolution and the blessing that is given. The first key is, of course, repentance. True repentance is also necessary for the Catholic to encounter the Lord in the sacrament.

REPENTANCE AS CONVERSION

The sacraments are the greatest gifts the Catholic has to overcome sin and yield to God's love. The sacrament of Reconciliation, in particular, is our opportunity to make true repentance. This repentance is the beginning of our deliverance from our own sinful patterns and from the influence of the enemy. Unfortunately, believers sometimes have inaccurate views of repentance. True repentance is not simply sorrow or regret that we have done wrong. Nor does true repentance entail trying harder to not repeat the same sins. Rather, repentance means *metanoia*, a changed or renewed mind that leads to a changed life.

Conversion is an essential aspect of this change. Pope John Paul II defined conversion as "making a personal decision about the saving sovereignty of Christ and becoming his disciple."[57] Many forms of evangelization fall short of conversion because they do not invite the person to make a decisive response to the message. We can give assent to the message, but externalize it as a truth to be respected, honored, or believed. Faith is more than just believing with one's mind; it is trusting with one's life. Faith is personal. It requires a grace-filled response to what God has revealed. God wants us to receive the truth by the power of the Holy Spirit in a way that transforms our lives.

In the Unbound Model, we emphasize listening to the person tell his story. After listening prayerfully and carefully, we help the struggling believer make a decisive response to the Gospel in the areas of his life where it has yet to penetrate. His response to the Lord in repentance and faith, forgiveness, and renunciation releases freedom.

REPENTANCE AS CONFESSION

Confession is another important aspect and a necessary expression of repentance. The sacrament of Reconciliation takes place, therefore, within the broader context of ongoing repentance and the life of faith. After one of our conferences, a woman who had received deliverance told me, "I drove right to church and made a deep confession of my sins." This woman took to heart the exhortation in Ephesians to live in the light:

> For once you were darkness, but now in the Lord you
> are light. Live as children of light — for the fruit of the

> light is found in all that is good and right and true. Try
> to find out what is pleasing to the Lord. Take no part
> in the unfruitful works of darkness, but instead expose
> them.
>
> — Eph 5: 8-11

As she exposed the works of darkness in her life, she was able to find what pleased the Lord.

But we find in Scripture that confession of sin should be communal as well as sacramental. In the letter of James, we are told to confess our sins to one another:

> Therefore confess your sins to one another, and pray
> for one another, that you may be healed. The prayer of
> a righteous man has great power in its effects.
>
> — Jas 5:16

This Scripture points to the sacrament of Reconciliation, but it also points beyond it, to the relationships we have in the Body of Christ. Sin takes place in relationship to others. When one member sins, the rest of the Body is wounded. Therefore, the struggle against sin is always relational as well, just as pursuing God takes place within the context of community.[58] Great healing takes place when we confess our sins to one another, and pray for one another. Standing as needy Christians, together at the foot of the cross, we will most clearly see the unity we have been given in Christ. From this position, it should neither be hard nor abnormal to ask forgiveness from one's spouse, fellow church member, or coworker.

Learning to pray with one another does not weaken the uniqueness of the sacrament but, rather, strengthens it. Yes, a sense of conviction about our sin prepares each of us to receive the sacramental graces of confession— but as we have seen, our repentance should be a part of the *daily* walk of faith. If evangelization is to be realized among the people of God, then lay people need to know how to help others make a personal expression of repentance and faith in Christ. Every Catholic should know how to lead his neighbor in a prayer of repentance and surrender to God. When the Unbound Model uses the terms "repentance and faith," it refers primarily to conversion, and secondarily to hidden sins of the heart that come to light and have not been confessed.

It is healthy for every believer to learn to confess his sins to God in prayer daily, rather than waiting until the sacrament is available. St. Ignatius of Loyola, in fact, encouraged the practice of daily examining one's conscience as one part of living a healthy spiritual life. Our call to evangelization includes helping another believer confess before God that she is in need of grace. As part of that, we help her extend forgiveness to all who have hurt her and renounce the lies that have held her bound. Finally, we teach her to stand in her authority as a child of God and resist the evil one (Jas 4:7). These are basic responses to the Gospel, part of our ongoing surrender to the Father's love in Christ. They should not be absent from the confessional nor from our daily devotions.

Unbound as Spiritual Direction

A good spiritual director helps a believer see the truth of what binds him and how the Lord is leading him. The director, with the help of the Holy Spirit, comes alongside the believer to guide him and to help him grow in deeper union with the Lord as he lives his Catholic faith. The Unbound Model has many similarities to spiritual direction. Like a good director, Unbound also seeks to uncover the lies of the enemy and the motives of the heart; and the model seeks to help each person to aggressively pursue the Lord in cooperation with the graces he has been given. Our model of deliverance places a priority on inviting specific verbal responses to the Gospel, which often lead to deeper conversion. It has been my experience that Catholics increase the practice of sacramental confessiononce they begin to see the battle that they face within their own souls and grow in awareness of their own responsibility for sinful patterns.

DELIVERANCE MINISTRY IN A PARISH SETTING

As the clergy and laity learn the principles of deliverance and begin to put them into practice, individual parishes will see an explosion of the life of Christ. In my travels, I have had the privilege of ministering in two parishes that have experienced the personal growth I believe will occur in parish after parish. Several years ago, my wife and I held a conference hosted by St. Michael's parish. After we had gone home, the pastor, Fr. Marc, wrote to us, bringing us up-to-date on the impact of the Unbound Model in his parish.

> We have been using the form of prayer you taught us. We completed the follow-up prayer for everybody signed up and the fruit has been remarkable. It is incredible to hear people say they feel free for the first time in their lives.
>
> Today, I went to visit a woman who has been admitted to hospice care. She is a very faith-filled woman and has accepted her cancer with courage, dignity and faith. I have prayed over her several times in the last year and half. Today I brought her communion. The minute I came through the door she brought up her ex-husband and all the bitterness and resentment she had and the hard time she had letting go of it. She said that the divorce happened fourteen years ago but it felt as if it was till fresh. She readily admitted that she had to forgive and she knew that the lack of forgiveness can often cause sickness in people. She half laughed and said maybe that's what happened to her.
>
> After her sharing and brief talk on what forgiveness really is, I shared with her what we learned in the conference about being set free in Christ. We went through the

process you taught us and then I prayed the prayer of command. This is what she said: "That's so weird, normally when you pray over me I feel something enter me. Just then I felt something go out of me. It felt like it left me from my stomach." She pointed near where her cancer started, in the colon, then smiled and said she never felt so free and never felt such joy in her heart.

Personally, I pray she has a miracle. But if not, she is at peace in freedom she never knew. Praise God.

The problem I have is that there is not enough time to pray with all those who need it. So I'm looking at starting a night of prayer in the Church every week with a team approach. Let freedom in Christ reign. Amen.

After three years of such ministry, Fr. Marc has become known for the help he brings to many. Now, the diocese refers to him people who may need deliverance ministry. He is a priest who is quite comfortable praying with parishioners inside the confessional. But Fr. Marc prefers the longer, more thorough approach when he senses there is an area of bondage. When he encounters someone whom he feels may benefit from more in-depth prayer, he gives them a penance of going over to the rectory and picking up a book called *Unbound*. He tells them that what they do with the teachings in the book is up to them, but if, after reading the first half, they wish to meet with him again, he will gladly accommodate them. Many have come back for prayer outside the confessional. On occasion, Fr. Marc will meet with a parishioner alone. At other times, he has a team with him who will pray for the person. When he offers the sacrament of Reconciliation during the session, he sends the team out of the room so he can hear the confession. In any case, his follow-up instructions always include encouragement to go to Mass and confessionregularly.

After our second conference in his parish, Fr. Marc shared more of his joy:

> It really was a great and beautiful conference. All were prayed for and I've heard how several individuals were set free. Praise God!!! Yesterday I met with a twenty-five year old man whom I know from marriage preparation. While sharing his life story he told how he was so bound up, moving inappropriately in sexual matters in his past as well as suffering from severe anxiety. After prayer, his words to me were, "I feel so new. Something big left me. I never want to go back there." He left a changed man and aware of the power of Christ's love. A great way to spend a Saturday afternoon!

Changed Lives

Just this year, I have seen how the Unbound teaching and prayer have changed lives in another parish. In this case, both the priest and the parishioners received great freedom. After our recent conference at St. Mary's, their pastor, Fr. Pierre, began to include the principles of Unbound in the confessional, but he did not stop there. He also prayed with a team outside of the sacrament. Let Fr. Pierre tell you about it in his own words.

> Last February, 2008, we had the *Unbound: Freedom in Christ* Conference in our parish, St. Mary's in Vancouver. I want to share what I have been experiencing since that time, as the parish priest of the community.

> For myself, I felt that a kind of sadness has been taken away from me. I am able to break free from some of my repetitive sins. I am more patient and forgiving of my

brothers in religious life. I pray to God, my Father, in a deeper and more constant way.

In my ministry of confession, I have been using a short form of the Unbound model. This has transformed "routine" confessions into meaningful ones. The penitents become more active. They no longer wait for advice and absolution. They discover for themselves whom they need to forgive, what they need to renounce, what is the lie in their lives. If there is a need, I use the fourth key, the command. I never had any manifestations of evil spirits. I am renewed through freedom in Christ, and so are the penitents. The focus is not evil spirits. I always use the fifth key, the blessing of the Father, after or with the form of absolution.

I also use the Unbound Model for spiritual direction. It gives me a framework to discern where the spiritual warfare is. The talk "Staying Free" by Ann Stevens is really helpful.

Finally, the talks by Neal Lozano about original sin and the devil's lie about our identity and God's identity has given me a simple and profound model to preach about spiritual warfare. It has given me tools to unmask the face of evil in our world, our culture, and our communities.

I am very grateful. Most of all, I am grateful that I discovered a way to help my parishioners receive the freedom Christ has already won for them. I can do more than offer a passive compassion. I can give them "tools" to deepen their relationship with Christ.

> I pray that Neal and Janet Lozano touch more priests and more parish communities.
>
> Fr. Pierre

Fr. Pierre took the principles of Unbound and incorporated them right away into the sacrament. He believed that in the context of the sacrament of Reconciliation, anything that separates one from God should be brought up. As the Catholic believer brings deeply buried attitudes and sins into the light, he is more and more able to receive the grace present in the sacrament. Once a Catholic has experienced the liberation available through deliverance ministry, he tends to turn more readily to a priest. Many Catholics originally come to an *Unbound: Freedom in Christ* conference because they remain in bondage despite repeated confession. Afterward, they seek out a priest, who lends his priestly role and presence to their faith as they express deep repentance for their offenses and renounce the lies that bind them to the sin that they have come to confess. Fr. Pierre discovered what we dream will be true in all parishes: the day of superficial confessions will be over; a new day of deep grace flowing from the sacrament of Reconciliation will be here.

CHAPTER 9

Restoring the Message of the Kingdom

For the kingdom of God does not consist in talk but in power.

— 1 Cor 4:20

In the summer of 1969, I spent a lot of time partying as I looked forward to returning to Villanova University for my junior year. Somewhere through the years, I had lost my way; at some point, I had lost my faith. I still went to church every Sunday, but I spent the time wondering why I was there and why other people were there. My thoughts for others were mostly negative judgments. I focused on those that stood out in overtly religious ways — viewing them as hypocrites. My thoughts about myself were about the emptiness I felt in the quiet reflective moments of the Mass and the deep unasked questions I carried, questions like "Why do I come every week to Mass?" and "Is there really a God?"

In August, my father entered the hospital with a bleeding esophagus, a result of liver failure caused by alcohol. In the days he spent in the hospital, I could not pray, for I thought the prayers of a sinner like me would not mean anything. God, if he existed, would hear the prayers of my mother and father, though, for they were faithful. But on August 29, my father died. Suddenly, my deep questions contracted into one big one: *Why?*

My dad was a good man. He was a good provider, never violent, a rock in the parish, and always ready to help the monsignor. He would either go to daily Mass or stop in to make a visit on his way to or from work. I know, because on those special days as a boy when I "went to work with Dad," we would stop in and say a prayer. I admired my dad. I still admire his goodness. His dad died when he was only two years old and, as the oldest boy, he took care of his mom. He was a friend to priests, and even had a lifelong friend who was a bishop. His faith was so important to him. After his death, we found a prayer card in his wallet that spoke of visiting Jesus in the Blessed Sacrament. He had carried that card with him since boyhood. He even attempted to evangelize one of my high school friends. Why would a man like that die when he was just fifty-three years old? Why had God not protected him?

My limited foundation of faith was not prepared to process the seeming contradiction between my father's death and a good God. I had already been losing parts of my father over the years to alcohol. Though I had grown, in the two years before his death, in understanding his problem, I never did understand why he could not stop drinking. Now he was gone. What he had failed to give me was now gone forever.

My question turned to anger. I watered the anger, and nourished it deep inside, until, eventually, I began to focus my anger on the possibility that there was no heaven, that what I had believed about life and death, heaven and hell was not just shallow, but a lie. My father was no place, and he had been cheated by the message of the Church, a message I no longer embraced. It is hard to believe that there is life after death if you carry emptiness and nothingness inside. Still, I went to Mass every Sunday.

Perhaps you, too, find yourself in church every Sunday, but are still empty inside. Perhaps you, too, find yourself saying the same things over and over at the sacrament of Reconciliation, but never see any lasting change in your heart. Priests throughout the Church know that there are so many who come to the sacraments and go away empty. Though the power for transformation is in the Eucharist, they too often see men and women unable to receive that power.[59] Bishop Kieran Conry, in an interview with the *Catholic Herald*, recognized the depth of our dilemma when he said, ". . . regular penitents came back with exactly the same words week after week. So there, you would say actually, there is no conversion taking place."[60]

CONVERSION

In a previous chapter I explained conversion as a change in mind and heart. It is the response we make when the truth of God's kingdom is proclaimed. We all are in need of conversion. Pope John Paul II said:

> The proclamation of the Word of God has *Christian conversion* as its aim: a complete and sincere adherence to Christ and his Gospel though faith.[61]

Conversion is a gift from God that "gives rise to a dynamic and lifelong process" that demands a continual turning away from "life according to the flesh" to "life according to the Spirit" (cf. Rom 8, 3-13).[62] The ability to live our life according to the Spirit, and not in bondage to our flesh, is afforded to every Catholic. How, then, do we convert? It begins, as the Pope has indicated, with the proclamation of the Word of God. St. Paul makes it clear that it is a proclamation with power.

> And I was with you in weakness and in much fear and trembling; and my speech and my message were not in plausible words of wisdom, but *in demonstration of the Spirit and of power,* that your faith might not rest in the wisdom of men but in the power of God.
>
> — 1 Cor 2:3-5 (emphasis added)

Five months after my father's death, I heard that proclamation with power. Standing in my childhood home, in the den where I had watched TV and wrestled with my brother, I asked my cousin, a priest, to explain the Mass to me again so I could get something out of it. I had asked the surface question. He answered the deeper question in his response.

"You will never know what is going on in Mass if you do not know God when you come to Mass," he said.

In that moment, stark reality overwhelmed me. I did not believe! A flood of objections arose from within: "But I went to Catholic school. I was an altar boy. I . . ." I thought, but didn't speak, these crumbling excuses. And a few moments later, my cousin began to pray. As he prayed, the answer that I had been searching for, the answer that I did not think could ever be known, came to me. The answer was a Person. In that den, Jesus revealed himself to me, and for the first time, I experienced the reality of his love and presence. That day, God met me in an encounter that changed my life.

I never tire of telling this story, for his mercy has persisted through the last forty years. Every trial, every challenge, every dry time, every form of willful stubborn resistance to God or sinful action, has ultimately been a doorway for me into deeper surrender. I had walked through conversion and found what my heart cried out for. I had found the life of Jesus.

If we have never had a moment in our life when we embraced the reality of the transforming power of baptism — if we have never had a moment when we accepted the saving work of Jesus and embraced him as Lord — there will remain a veil over the sacrament of Reconciliation and over the Eucharist. The One to whom we are being reconciled will be hidden. If we enter into the sacraments without a personal conversion toward his love, we cannot hear his message of love and forgiveness. Instead, we will hear another message of guilt, condemnation, and failure; we will remain in bondage to the lie that our willpower and our fresh resolve will save us.

Demonstration of the Spirit and of Power

The proclamation of the word of God never comes through words alone, for the life of Jesus is not found in mere words. It is found in the Word himself — the very Presence of Jesus who has promised to never leave us, never forsake us. He promises us, as he promised his disciples, his Holy Spirit.

> And while staying with them he charged them not to depart from Jerusalem, but to wait for the promise of the Father, which, he said, "you heard from me, for John baptized with water, but before many days you shall be baptized with the Holy Spirit."
>
> — Acts 1:4-5

Our God is a God who makes promises and then keeps them. He reveals himself as we wait upon the fulfillment of his promises. If the promise is missing from the proclamation, we have no expectation for what the Holy Father calls "a dynamic and lifelong process" leading to "life according to the Holy Spirit."

What is life in the Holy Spirit? It is a life of freedom. Sacred Scripture tells us, "Where the Spirit of the Lord is, there is freedom" (2 Cor 3:17). This is the promise we have received: "You will know the truth, and the truth will make you free" (Jn 8:32. The truth of knowing the Father and the Son and the Holy Spirit sets us free to be who we were originally intended to be — children of God. Galatians 5:1 tells us that it is "for freedom Christ has set us free." This freedom is the conversion to which we have been called. This freedom is at the heart of the proclamation we make. Jesus does not simply make a difference in the next life; for those who believe, he transforms everything in this life as well. When the promised Spirit of Christ takes the message of God and applies it to our deepest wounds and our most fervent longings, then the power of Jesus' life breaks out in us.

How can we be satisfied with repainting the outside when the Lord is offering us an "extreme makeover"? Do we really want to keep making mud pies in a puddle — as author and scholar C. S. Lewis suggests — when the Lord offers us the mighty ocean?

Unfortunately, if we are ruthlessly honest, many of us must admit that yes, we are satisfied with a smaller life. We have wanted only the good that Jesus could bring, rather than the life of Jesus himself. We have wanted the Spirit's gifts of wisdom or faith, rather than the Holy Spirit himself. The gifts and the good the Lord brings are a blessing to us, but only an encounter with the Lord of Life himself brings power that transforms the human heart. As the pope said, a "radically changed existence" comes when we believe that the "risen Jesus lives with me and in me."[63] As we daily practice the Presence of the Lord in our lives by inviting him in to each and every part — our talents and abilities, our goods and possessions, our relationships and influences — the power of the life of God will flow into us, through us, and from us.

THE KINGDOM OF GOD — JESUS' FIRST PROMISE

The first words of Jesus in Mark's Gospel are, "The time is fulfilled, and the kingdom of God is at hand; repent, and believe in the gospel"(Mk 15:1). In his book *Jesus of Nazareth*, Pope Benedict XVI reminds us that "the 'Kingdom of God' is a theme that runs through the whole of Jesus' teaching."[64] This was his message. Jesus taught us to pray for the Kingdom to come on earth as it is in heaven. Jesus continues by his Spirit to bring the Kingdom. The Holy Father tells us, "Through Jesus' presence and *action* (my emphasis), God has here and now entered actively into history in a wholly new ways."[65] And one of the actions of Jesus is the driving out of demons.

> But if it is by the finger (Spirit) of God that I cast out
> demons, then the kingdom of God has come upon
> you.
>
> — Lk 11:20

Referring to this Scripture, the Holy Father continues:

> It is not simply in Jesus' physical presence that "Kingdom"
> is located; rather, it is in his action, accomplished by the
> Holy Spirit.[66]

Healing, deliverance, and exorcism are manifestations of Jesus' presence. He is revealed in his actions. These are ways he shows his love, just as he did in the New Testament when he treated the poor with dignity, healed the sick, and set the oppressed free. Jesus conquered the evils of sickness, suffering, and all forms of torment as he proclaimed the Gospel of the Kingdom.

It is tempting to place the healing and comfort of the Kingdom into the afterlife, but the Holy Father makes it clear that the grace of the Kingdom is with us now:

> Jesus' many healings clearly show his great compassion
> in the face of human distress, *but they also signify that in
> the kingdom there will no longer be sickness or suffering,
> and that his mission, from the very beginning, is meant to
> free people from these evils.*[67]

The message of the Kingdom confronts the evils of the kingdom of darkness and exposes their source. The message of the Kingdom of God, invading earth through Jesus Christ, reveals that there is a battle in which we play a significant role: the battle between the advancing Kingdom of God and the kingdom of darkness that Jesus came to destroy.

Two *KERYGMAS*

Jesus' own message, or *kerygma*, was clear: he came to usher in the Kingdom of God. His disciples also had a *kerygma*: that the

"Christ-event" — the birth, death, and resurrection of Jesus Christ — shows the greatness of the love of God for us. Pope John Paul II believed that it was critical for the Church to unite the two *kerygmas*.

> The preaching of the early Church was centered on the proclamation of Jesus Christ, with whom the Kingdom was identified. Now, as then, there is a need to unite the proclamation of the Kingdom of God (the content of Jesus' own *kerygma*) and the proclamation of the Christ-event (the *kerygma* of the apostles). The two proclamations are complementary; each throws light on the other.[68]

It is no small thing to proclaim the life-transforming message of the love of God revealed in the person Jesus Christ. But the message of the Kingdom brings new light and power to the proclamation of God's saving love. Proclaiming the Gospel of the Kingdom does not simply mean using the vocabulary that Jesus used about the Kingdom; it requires personal identification with Christ and his mission. We move from encountering Christ into identification with him and doing what he did. He did whatever he saw the Father doing. As we know from the letter of John, "The reason the Son of God appeared was to destroy the works of the devil" (1 Jn 3:8b). This is the foundation by which we understand the restoration of exorcism and deliverance ministry in the Church.

Through the oils of baptism, we have slipped free of the enemy's grasp; through the waters of baptism, we have died to our old selves that lived under Satan's rule. And now, we must progressively die to his empty promises and all the works we have done under his influence. Since we have been delivered from the kingdom of darkness and are now in God's Kingdom, we acknowledge God's dominion, his lordship, over every part of our lives. We must turn our backs on — renounce — every work of ours that carries the smoke of hell. As we submit to "the Lord's lordship," we will be full of joy.

But our joy is not complete unless we impart the Kingdom. St. John wrote his first Epistle so that his joy would be complete (1 Jn 1:4). Thus, he shared God's message of love with us. Our joy is complete when we give our message away — when the Kingdom of God manifests in the lives of those who hear. It is our responsibility to proclaim the message of the Kingdom. Expectation for healing, deliverance, and exorcism is part of the restoration of the Gospel of the Kingdom. It is very exciting to contemplate, because the proclamation of the Kingdom will be one of the signs that the return of the Lord is approaching.

> And this gospel of the kingdom will be preached throughout the whole world, as a testimony to all nations; and then the end will come.
>
> — Mt 24:14

The more we understand the Kingdom and proclaim it with power, the greater its advance, and the nearer we are to Christ's return.

We can never forget that both exorcism and deliverance ministry take place in the context of the dynamic process leading us to freedom in Christ. Breaking free from the enemy's lies — breaking out of areas of bondage or even out of possession — is just the beginning. It is a breakthrough into the normal Christian life moving from testing to victory, from struggle to rejoicing, from fasting to feasting, and from death to life.

THE KINGDOM MADE KNOWN

On a wintry December afternoon, as I listened to my phone messages from the day before, one caught my attention.

"This is Fr. Joseph. I have some urgent questions to ask you."

Fr. Joseph had just finished a brief meeting with a young man and some members of the man's prayer group. He had promised to pray with Ricardo the next day. Reflecting later on what he had heard, he became concerned and a bit nervous about what he had promised.

Ricardo, a recent immigrant from Latin America, was staying temporarily with a local family while he adjusted to life in the United States. The family, however, found him to be out of control. He exhibited wild rebelliousness, accompanied by drinking and staying out all night. As the American family tried to pray with him, he manifested demonically. His eyes rolled back into his head and he blacked out. One night, they found him on the roof, unable to either get off nor explain how he got there. As far as the family could see, his presence on the roof was impossible, unless some superhuman force had aided him.

The family contacted the bishop, believing that he needed an exorcism. At the bishop's recommendation, they came to Fr. Joseph who, though not an exorcist, does regularly pray with people as part of his ministry. In a brief interview, he discovered that Ricardo had encounters with the devil. He had invited the devil to "show me who you are and what power you have." Another time, he asked the devil to come into him and help him.

Fr. Joseph left a lot of questions on the answering machine. "Do you think he needs an exorcism? Do you think it is safe to pray with him? I have intercessors, but no man to hold him down if something happens. What if he has superhuman strength? What if he attacks me? What if he is truly possessed?"

Now, I had met Fr. Joseph several times; he had studied the Unbound Model for deliverance and had had success helping people using the principles, but he had never faced someone who had consciously opened his life to the devil. Since I was not able to get back to him before the appointment, Fr. Joseph committed the whole situation to the Lord and his protection.

Fr. Joseph was calm as he interviewed the young man, seeking to discover the various ways that the devil may have gained access into his life. While he listened to Ricardo's story, he listed all the things that Ricardo might need to renounce, not stopping at the obvious invitation to Satan. He also included anything that may have led Ricardo to this place, such as his father's absence during childhood and the pains of growing up. Then he began to apply the five keys of Unbound.

Repentance and faith, the first key, is something Fr. Joseph understood (long before he met me) and explained at that point to Ricardo. Ricardo needed to choose Jesus to be his Lord and Savior. Fr. Joseph carefully explained the plan for salvation: that the Gospel is a story of God's love, and that God wanted to set him free and give him a new life. He explained how sin is a barrier to God's love, and that the only way to break free is through the love of God revealed in Jesus. He told Ricardo that Jesus died for his sins and made a way for him to come freely to the Father. Finally, he told him he needed to make a decision to ask Jesus to be Lord and decide to follow him.

Fr. Joseph also knew how important it was for Ricardo to express that verbally. Words have power to express the deep workings of the Spirit within. Our words express our agreement with the Holy Spirit, who is leading us to Jesus. Our agreement, our submission, expresses our faith that becomes a door by which the power of the Holy Spirit is released. But in this case, there was one more element that Fr. Joseph also understood. Ricardo's words would be heard by his enemies; they would act like a sledgehammer, striking the claim and breaking the plans the evil one had for his life. So Fr. Joseph spent considerable time explaining the Gospel, wanting to be sure Ricardo understood the decision he was asking the young man to make. He finished with a question.

"Are you sure you want to make this decision?"

"Yes, yes," Ricardo answered.

At that point, Fr. Joseph invited Ricardo to receive the sacrament of Reconciliation, encouraging him to tell the sins that he was most afraid to tell anyone about. Because he was alone with the man (the intercessors were in the next room), Fr. Joseph was free to take Ricardo through the rest of the keys of Unbound within the sacrament. When Ricardo finished confessing his sins, Fr. Joseph led him to pronounce forgiveness over those who had hurt him, rejected him, or abandoned him. Then he led Ricardo to renounce the authority that he gave the devil when he asked him to come into his life. Next. Fr. Joseph led Ricardo to renounce each lie he believed about himself and God, every area of agreement with the enemy.

Following Ricardo's renunciations, Father gave the man absolution for his sins and incorporated the fourth key of command: "In the name of Jesus, I command every evil spirit that Ricardo renounced to leave now."

Did Ricardo experience freedom at that point? Fr. Joseph knew that he could continue with the interview, with deeper renunciation and forgiveness, if he had not. But once Ricardo expressed a sense of freedom, Fr. Joseph moved on to the fifth key of the Unbound Model, the Father's Blessing. By blessing Ricardo, Fr. Joseph allowed Jesus to bring him to God the Father to have his true identity and life's purpose affirmed and restored. It was in this affirmation and restoration that Ricardo's heart was healed. The priest ended by speaking the priestly blessing over Ricardo.

What was the impact on the troubled young man? Fr. Joseph told me that Ricardo left his office filled with joy, eager to come to Bible study, and eager to see him again. He wanted to build on the release of the power of Christ and the power of his baptism.

Whether the keys are applied within the sacrament or outside, in conjunction with repentance and sacrament coming later, isn't important. What is important is that the Kingdom of God — the action of God — is released to do what the Gospel is meant to do.

The Rhythm of Catholic Life

On the day of my initial conversion, I left my anger behind. I knew then that my father was with the Lord, and that one day, by God's grace, I would see him again. My Dad gave me something through his death that he could not give me in his life. When I heard the message and received it in power, gratitude overwhelmed my anger. Through the years I have had other life-altering encounters with the Lord where, after a season of testing, he came, revealing his love and changing my heart. This has been my personal experience of the Kingdom made known in the person of Christ. But even more than this, I have seen the power of God set captives free. Having learned the principles of the five keys, I have been able to teach them in many countries and cities.

These keys are becoming part of the rhythm of Catholic life in many places, as they find expression in priests like Fr. Pierre, who uses them in the confessional as well as in his preaching and spiritual direction. They are bringing new life to the Church as they are used by priests like Fr. Joseph, who is growing confident in the promises of the Gospel, greeting those tormented by fear and carefully using the gift of deliverance ministry, along with the sacrament of Reconciliation, to lead people out of bondage into conversion. The keys are confronting the deepest sins, as a priest like Fr. Francis — dedicated to receiving people with respect and getting them the help they need — prepares to enter into the battle for the lives of those who are possessed and in need of a major exorcism. And the grace worked through the keys is flowering as priests like Fr. Longins of Rwanda, who trained more than 100 lay people to train others in the five keys, begin to show their own lay people how to help those in spiritual bondage.

The ministry of the laity is powerful. After my friend Carolina was set free of bondage to fear, she was filled with compassion and understanding. Now, under her pastor's guidance, she prays every week with the Unbound Model for people who call for help. I know many Carolinas; it is my hope that every exorcist would have Carolinas close to him who can use the keys of non-confrontational deliverance to set people free from bondage. Let the exorcist be freed to spend his precious time with those who are truly possessed.

I also pray that every priest would have members of his parish who are actively evangelizing, proclaiming the Kingdom in its power. Then, when his parishioners come to confession, they would come prepared, having engaged their minds, their wills, and their hearts, ready to fully receive the grace that awaits them in the sacraments.

In the early Church, on the vigil of Easter, those to be baptized stood before the community of believers and declared that they renounced Satan and all of his works and all of his empty promises. The Church has preserved this practice for us. It is part of the baptismal rite renewed publicly every year. It is our inheritance. As the sacrament of Reconciliation is the renewal of baptism, renunciation also has a place within this sacrament. Evangelization and the expectancy of God's promises open the door to victory over all the works of the enemy and to healing for our souls through sacramental absolution.

There are too many very good Catholics, like my dad, who suffer with compulsive and addictive behaviors. There are too many good Catholics who have yet to really hear the message of the Kingdom and the promises contained in the Gospel. Too many Catholics don't expect the life-changing encounters with the Lord that have been promised to those who believe. But the

Heavenly Father has promised us life in the Spirit. If only we would ask, we will receive.

> "If you then, who are evil, know how to give good gifts to your children, how much more will the heavenly Father give the Holy Spirit to those who ask him!"
>
> — Lk 11:13

Nothing can come close to the restoration that comes through the dynamic work of the Holy Spirit — drawing us, through the Savior, to know the Father who loves us. Nothing can come close to the joy of knowing that we have come as God's children to an eternal home that will never be shaken.

I thought my dad took with him that which I needed to his grave; in truth, my dad opened the door for me to know and receive the Father's love and the promise that there is more. There is always more freedom for the children of God.

Appendix A

The Imperative Command and the Laity

Since Vatican II, there has been a heightened awareness of the Holy Spirit working though the whole people of God by means of various charisms. With this awareness has come the growth of deliverance ministries. Though Church exorcists and those in deliverance ministry fight the same foe, they often look at similar spiritual realities from different perspectives. This has brought healthy tension to ministry, along with a need for dialogue and clarification.

One of the questions for anyone involved in deliverance ministry today is, "Can anyone other than a priest legitimately use the imperative?" That is, can just anyone vocally command an evil spirit to leave?

Because real or perceived abuses have occurred in both exorcism and deliverance, the Church has taken time to set clear boundaries on the public ministry of the Church by establishing the Rite of Exorcism. Unfortunately, this has caused some confusion for the laity, who may inappropriately apply the Church's direction regarding public ministry to private ministry. Recognition of past abuses, along with a proper interpretation of Church teaching on public and private ministry, will enable us to understand the appropriate role of the laity in deliverance ministry — specifically, the proper use of the imperative.

New Testament Teaching on Casting out Demons

Chapter Four explained how the Church's original charism of casting out demons fell into disuse, apart from the service of the exorcists. Over the last fifty years, however, that charism has reemerged as many have looked back at the teachings of Jesus and the example of the early Church. Many in the Church have come to realize that Jesus' mission to set the captives free (Lk 4:18-19) and destroy the works of the enemy (1 Jn 3:8) is our mission as well. It is the mission of the Church and of every believer.

We see that casting out of spirits is a charism of the Holy Spirit. The Twelve were the first to receive this charism:

> And he called the twelve together and gave them power and authority over all demons and to cure diseases.
>
> — Lk 9:1

Soon after, Jesus gave this same power to the seventy disciples:

> "Behold, I have given you authority to tread upon serpents and scorpions, and over all the power of the enemy; and nothing shall hurt you."
>
> — Lk 10:19

Finally, the risen Lord broadens this gift to all who follow him:

> "And these signs will accompany those who believe: in my name they will cast out demons; they will speak in new tongues."
>
> — Mk 16:17

The power Jesus received from his Father he passed on to all who believe in his name through his promised Holy Spirit. After the resurrection, he instructed his disciples to "stay in the city, until you are clothed with power from on high" (Lk 24:49). This power was released on all the disciples at Pentecost. The result of being baptized in the Holy Spirit was the release of power (Acts 1:8). Is not this the same power available to us to come to the aid of those who are afflicted? The early Church Fathers thought so. They understood that ordinary Christians had this power. Tertullian (AD 197-220) wrote that the casting out of demons was one of the pleasures God has given the Christian:

> What nobler than to tread underfoot the gods of the nations — to exorcise evil spirits — to perform cures — to seek divine revealings — to live to God? These are the pleasures, these the spectacles that befit Christian men — holy, everlasting, free.[69]

One clear indication we have that Jesus — far from restricting the charism of casting out demons — expected it to be widely used was his response to his disciples' protest that a man not of their number was casting out spirits in his name. They wanted to stop the man; Jesus was quite clear that the man should not be prevented from doing such a mighty work:

> John said to him, "Teacher, we saw a man casting out demons in your name, and we forbade him, because he was not following us." But Jesus said, "Do not forbid him; for no one who does a mighty work in my name will be able soon after to speak evil of me. For he that is not against us is for us."
>
> — Mk 9:38-40

The Christians of the first three centuries referred to the use of this charism simply as the casting out of the evil spirits. They did not use any formal ritual, just spoke in the holy name of Jesus, only gradually adding the Sign of the Cross and, in some cases, exsufflation (breathing on the afflicted person). Over time, however, the Church developed the ritual in order to provide for the afflicted through its official ministry. With the ritual came the use of the term "exorcist" to describe one who carries out the official warfare of the Church against evil spirits.

The word *exorcism* comes from the Greek *exorkizein*, meaning "to cast out a demon by adjuration." *Adjure*, used three times in the New Testament, means to solemnly command or put under oath.[70] It is not hard to connect the dots here: Following the example of Scripture, we command evil spirits to leave. The "command" is an essential part of what we mean by exorcism.

In 1641, the Rite of Exorcism was established as a public ministry of the Church. Since the sacred rite is only to be used by the priest at the permission of the bishop, the use of the imperative (commanding a demon, in the name of Jesus Christ, to leave) became, in the minds of many Catholics, erroneously restricted to the clergy. Since there is a great desire on the part of Catholics to be under authority and not to go beyond any practice limited by the Church, many lay people will discontinue ministry rather than breach what they think is the teaching of the Church.

But has the Church really restricted the command?

In 1984, in response to inquiries from bishops about gatherings that focused on deliverance from the influence of demons, then-Cardinal Ratzinger, prefect of the Congregation for the Doctrine of the Faith, wrote the "Letter to Local Ordinaries on Some Prescriptions Concerning Exorcism," reproduced below.

> *Excellency,*
>
> *For some years there has been an increase in the number of ecclesial gatherings which seek liberation from demonic influences, even though they are not properly and truly exorcisms. These groups, even when a priest is present, are lead by lay persons.*
>
> *Since the Congregation of the Doctrine of the Faith has been asked what ought to be thought about this, this dicastery is of the opinion that all other ordinaries should have the following response:*
>
> *Canon 1172 of the Code of Canon law declares that no one is able to legitimately undertake exorcisms of the possessed unless expressed and individual permission has been obtained from the ordinary of the place (†1). The canon also establishes that this permission ought to be conceded by the ordinary of the place only to priests who are distinguished by piety, knowledge, prudence, and integrity of life (†2). Bishops are, therefore, strongly urged to see to the observance of these norms.*
>
> *From these prescriptions it follows, therefore, that no member of the Christian faithful can use formula for exorcism against Satan and fallen angels, extracted from that which was made law by Leo XIII, and even less are they able to use the entire text for exorcism. Bishops are to bring this to the attention of the faithful as it is deemed necessary.*
>
> *Finally, for these same reasons, bishops are asked to be vigilant that — for even cases in which a true diabolical*

possession is excluded, diabolical influence nevertheless seems in some way to be revealed — those who do not have the required faculty not serve in the leading of meetings where, in order to gain freedom, prayers are used which dignify demons by directly questioning them and in searching to make known their identity.

The announcement of these norms, however, ought not keep the faithful from praying that, as Jesus taught us, they might be delivered from evil (cf. Mt. 6:13). Finally, pastors ought to avail themselves of this occasion to recall what the tradition of the Church teaches about the proper function of the sacraments and the intercession of the Blessed Virgin Mary, the angels and the saints in the spiritual fight of Christians against evil spirits.[71]

Yours in Christ
Joseph Card. Ratzinger
Prefect
+ Alberto Bovone
Titular Archbishop of Cesarea di Numidia
Secretary

It is easy to see why many faithful Catholics believe that only a priest should use the imperative command. Fortunately, leaders among the clergy have received unambiguous clarification regarding these activities, and we are now able to interpret these documents with wisdom.

The key to clearing up the confusion is understanding the distinction between public and private ministry. A "public" ministry refers to the public presentation or representation of the Church's ministry. Lay people are not to represent themselves as those who have public ministries, as if those ministries are representative of the bishop. They are not to lead assemblies for the purpose of deliverance as if they do it on the bishop's behalf. They must be clear that they do not speak in the name of the Church unless officially designated to do so by the bishop.

When we pray, we speak in our own name, and call on the name of Jesus. In the same way, "private" ministry is not one that is conducted in isolation, but rather a ministry that is distinct from a public assembly of the official Church.

Fr. Francis Martin clarified the cardinal's letter in a talk at Mundelein Seminary, and later through personal correspondence. He stated that it is clear that the restrictions in point three of Cardinal Ratzinger's letter apply to public assemblies. He also wrote:

> When asked by Fr. Rufus Pereira concerning the third paragraph of Statement of the Congregation of the Doctrine of the Faith, September 19, 1984, the then-Prefect of the Congregation, Cardinal Joseph Ratzinger, replied that the restriction applied to public assemblies.[72]

While Cardinal Ratzinger (now Pope Benedict XVI) clearly restricts exorcisms and prayers for exorcism to authorized clergy, there is nothing here that prohibits the laity from using the imperative. "Exorcisms" refers to the Rite of Exorcism — a sacramental, not the imperative command. His first point reminds bishops of Canon 1172 regarding the Rite of Exorcism:

> Can. 1172 §1. No one can perform exorcisms legitimately upon the possessed unless he has obtained special and express permission from the local ordinary.

Therefore, when Cardinal Ratzinger prohibits lay exorcisms, he is referring to the performance of the official rite.

Ratzinger's second point refers to the formula of Pope Leo XIII. Again, he prohibits lay use of an official Church formula only.[73]

In his third point, Ratzinger specifically forbids the organizing of meetings "during which, for the purpose of deliverance, such prayers are used to directly invoke demons and where their identity is sought." When the people of God gather, Jesus Christ should be the center; invoking demons or provoking them to manifest in public assemblies is not the way the Church should gather.

These restrictions placed on public assemblies and ministry do not apply to private ministry unless the local bishop, for pastoral reasons, places restrictions on such activity. Although the word of command that is used in deliverance ministry can bear resemblance to the commands used by a priest in a public exorcism, they are not the same because the context is different. However, although the Church has not restricted the imperative command to clergy, it remains true that there is a need for sound pastoral guidance and teaching for both deliverance ministry and the work of the exorcist.

Confusion Removed Further: The Primacy of Rome and the Role of the Local Bishops

The Church has the authority and responsibility to regulate all public ministry. Rome has a particular responsibility regarding the Rite of Exorcism. The Pope himself, however, clarified that responsibility when he was still Cardinal Ratzinger:

> To me it would be a mistaken conception of the primacy, if Rome had to correct everything. No, Rome must commit herself, together with the college of bishops, to see to it that there are shepherds who all rally together and in the great communion of the saints and in responsibility before the Lord, act in fear of the Lord, not out of fear of men. They must act together to make possible a faith that is free.[74]

Local diocesan bishops have responsibility to see that the Rite of Exorcism is properly used and not abused. They also have responsibility to oversee all public ministries, such as deliverance ministries, that are, in my view, outside of the scope of the Rite of Exorcism. To appeal to Rome to regulate private ministry is a mistake. Local bishops have the responsibility to teach and lead their dioceses and to implement Church directives with pastoral care.

The Appeal to Scripture and the *Catechism*

The idea that only clergy can command demons to leave is also difficult to reconcile with Scripture. From the Scriptures quoted at the beginning of the appendix, it is clear that Jesus expects his disciples — all who proclaim the message of the Kingdom of God — to exercise the gift (charism) of casting out demons. In fact, Jesus appears frustrated at one point with his disciples for not speaking a word of command with faith. Having failed to set a demonized boy free the disciples asked Jesus, "Why could we not cast it out?" His answer did not have to do with authority or power; they already had that. The issue was faith.

> And when they came to the crowd, a man came up to him and kneeling before him said, "Lord, have mercy on my son, for he is an epileptic and he suffers terribly; for often he falls into the fire, and often into the water. And I brought him to your disciples, and they could not heal him." And Jesus answered, "O faithless and perverse generation, how long am I to be with you? How long am I to bear with you? Bring him here to me." And Jesus rebuked him, and the demon came out of him, and the boy was cured instantly. Then the disciples came to Jesus privately and said, "Why could we not cast it out?" He said to them, "Because of your little faith. For truly, I say to you, if you have faith as a grain of mustard seed, you will say to this mountain, 'Move from here to there,' and it will move; and nothing will be impossible to you."
>
> — Mt 17:14-20

Moreover, the risen Lord promises that signs of the presence and power of the Kingdom, including the casting out of demons, will accompany those who believe in him:

> "These signs will accompany those who believe: in my name they will cast out demons; they will speak in new tongues; they will pick up serpents, and if they drink any deadly thing, it will not hurt them; they will lay their hands on the sick, and they will recover."
>
> — Mk. 16:17-18[75]

Now, what is the difference between the authority given by Jesus to all his disciples and the authority exercised in the Rite of Exorcism? The *Catechism* makes a very clear distinction between that which is public, and therefore reserved for the clergy, and that which is private and available to all believers:

> When the Church asks *publicly and authoritatively* in the name of Jesus Christ that a person or object be protected against the power of the Evil One and withdrawn from his dominion, it is called exorcism. Jesus performed exorcisms (Mk 1:25 ff.) and from him the Church has received the power and office of exorcising (Mk 3:15; 6:7,13; 16:17). In a simple form, exorcism is performed at the celebration of baptism. The *solemn exorcism, called 'a major exorcism,' can be performed only by a priest and with the permission of the bishop.* The priest must proceed with prudence, strictly observing the rules established by the Church.
>
> — *CCC* 1673 (emphasis added).

Fr. Jeffrey Grob, who has served as the Associate Vicar for Canonical Services and assistant to the Exorcist for the Archdiocese of Chicago, states:

> An exorcism is considered "public" when an authorized person using an approved rite does it in the name of the Church. A "private" exorcism is not bound by the same constraints and may be celebrated by any of the faithful.[76]

The Appeal to the Church Fathers

It is clear from the writings of the early Church Fathers that the charism of casting out demons was not only commonplace but an expected part of the life of a Christian disciple. The power to cast out demons was given to all Christians, men and women. St. Cyprian of Carthage (c. AD 250) taught that this power is made available to the Christian at the moment of baptism.

> But when such people come forward to receive the waters of salvation and the sanctification of baptism, we ought to be convinced and firmly believe that the devil is there overpowered and that through God's mercy the man now dedicated to Him is set free.[77]

St. Cyprian recognized, however, that though freedom may come initially, it was possible for a Christian to fall again under the devil's influence. Why is that? St. Cyprian answered:

> Hence we can plainly see that in baptism the devil is driven out by faith of the believer and that he comes back again if that faith should subsequently falter.[78]

St. Cyprian ties the power to fight the devil to the faith of the individual believer. Active faith releases the power provided through baptism, much as turning on a light switch releases the flow of electricity to light a house. Whether a believer's baptism took place yesterday or fifty years ago, the same power was present in the sacrament. Each Christian — man or woman, old or young, cleric or layperson — must have the living faith to access that power. Jesus said to his disciples:

> "I say to you, if you have faith as a grain of mustard seed, you will say to this mountain, 'Move hence to yonder place,' and it will move; and nothing will be impossible to you."
>
> — Mt 17:20

In these words, Jesus gives powerful authority to his disciples. The baptized believer needs to know that he has this authority over his enemies; he needs to be strengthened in his faith so that he can take his stand against the evil one, for it is by the "faith of the believer" that the devil is driven out.

The confusion over the imperative form has proved to be an obstacle to faith for some, as they relinquish their own responsibility to put their faith in the Christ who alone can save them from their troubles. The Church's role is not to fight the battle but to build up the faith of the believer, so that he can command his enemy to leave. The struggle for clarification of the authority to command the enemy to leave is a process that sharpens our discernment and calls us all to yield to the gift of humility. But it is clear that speaking the word of command is a gift God wants his people to have the faith to use as he brings release to those in bondage.

Understanding the Work of Evil Spirits

In this book, I have placed the focus on the struggle against the influence of evil spirits. While it is true that "the devil is not the cause of every sin . . . but some are due to the free will and the corruption of the flesh,"[79] it is also true that the testimony of Sacred Scripture and the Catechism together make it clear that evil spirits operate behind sin, particularly when the sin involves the worship of anything other than the Lord.

In Deuteronomy, Moses tells the Israelites that when they abandoned God, and rejected the "Rock of [their] salvation" (32:15), they, in fact, "sacrificed to demons which were no gods, to gods they had never known, to new gods that had come in of late, whom your fathers had never dreaded" (32:17). In 1 Corinthians 10:20-21, St. Paul says:

> No, I imply that what pagans sacrifice they offer to demons and not to God. I do not want you to be partners with demons. You cannot drink the cup of the Lord and the cup of demons. You cannot partake of the table of the Lord and the table of demons.

Again, it is clear that any worship not directed at the Lord God Almighty is, in fact, worship of a demon.

The Church has always understood that our battle is "against the principalities, against the powers, against the world rulers of this present darkness, against the spiritual hosts of wickedness in the heavenly places" (Eph 6:12). The *Catechism* picks up on this when it says:

> The whole of man's history has been the story of our combat with the powers of evil, stretching, so our Lord tells us, from the very dawn of history until the last day.
>
> — *CCC* 409

The *Catechism* further acknowledges the great struggle man faces to "do what is right, and at great cost to himself," recognizing that the fight against evil involves a fight against the effects of original sin within man as well as a fight against the influence of evil spirits. Since spiritual warfare properly entails a balance between outer and inner struggle, it is important for us to understand the work of evil spirits.

WHAT WE MEAN BY A "SPIRIT," OR ANGELS AND DEMONS

Much of what we know about demons, or evil spirits, comes from what we know about angels. Angels and demons are both spirits created by God. Demons are angels that sinned, rebelling against God by forsaking their true identity as worshipers and servants of God.

> For if God did not spare the angels when they sinned, but cast them into hell and committed them to pits of nether gloom to be kept until the judgment . . .
>
> — 2 Pet 2:4

> And the angels that did not keep their own position but left their proper dwelling have been kept by him in eternal chains in the nether gloom until the judgment of the great day.
>
> — Jude 1:6

To properly understand evil spirits, it is instructive to look, then, at what the Scriptures say about angels.

First, angels sometimes appear in human form. The letter to the Hebrews instructs us to show hospitality for this very reason:

> Do not forget to entertain strangers, for by so doing some people have entertained angels without knowing it.
>
> — Heb 13:2 (*NIV*)

Perhaps we entertain demons without knowing it as well. St. Paul warns Timothy about "giving heed to deceitful spirits and doctrines of demons" (1 Tim 4:1). False doctrines can be inspired by evil spirits.

Another revealing Scripture about angels is in Jesus' comment about children, in which he references guardian angels:

> "See that you do not despise one of these little ones; for I tell you that in heaven their angels always behold the face of my Father who is in heaven."
>
> — Mt 18:10

Angels are able to behold the Father in heaven and, at the same time, help us.

> Are they not all ministering spirits sent to serve, for the sake of those who are to inherit salvation?
>
> — Heb 1:14 (*NAB*)

How do they do this? Spirits do not have bodies, so time and matter do not restrain them in any way. Instead of going to a place physically, they are able to "go" by spiritually focusing their thoughts. Angels see the face of the Father while they minister to us; they are spiritually present wherever they focus their thoughts. Because angels focus on God first, their ministry to us always flows from this eternal vision. As they focus then on us, they carry to us what they have seen in God. Even more, they do so in freedom. They always choose to obey God, the one who sends them forth as his messengers. But as free beings with a free will,[80] they also can choose to help us. The *Catechism* says:

> Freedom is the power to act or not to act, and so to perform deliberate acts of one's own. Freedom attains perfection in its acts when directed toward God, the sovereign Good.
>
> — CCC 1744

Since angels have the power to act or not, it is good to ask angels for assistance, as we do when we pray to St. Michael the Archangel to defend us in our battle against evil.

Our battle is against spirits that have fallen. Their primary focus is on themselves and their eternal torment. Out of this dark focus, their "eternal chains," they roam about and harass us. They bring to us not the life of God, but the purposelessness, loneliness, isolation, and hatred of God that consumes them as they continually and compulsively contemplate their eternal emptiness. We are properly warned by St. Peter:

> Be sober, be watchful. Your adversary the devil prowls around like a roaring lion, seeking some one to devour.
>
> — 1 Pet 5:8

How Spirits Work

The thoughts angels send our way flow from their contemplation of God and their communication with God. Angels bring to us the truth that reveals the God of love. They bring images and thoughts that attract us to God and help us on the path of salvation. Angels are freely attracted to God and the things of God; they want to impart to us their love and attraction to God and the things of God. They know our true nature and that our destiny is to share in God's divine life. They are God's messengers, his servants seeking to bring us into our destiny. They are committed to this plan and want to advance God's will. If the focus of Jesus' ministry was to do the Father's will by advancing the Kingdom, we can presume that angels, who are continually in worship before God, are about the same work. "They serve those who will inherit salvation" (Heb 1:14).

Demons serve only themselves and the devil's purposes. Their thoughts are always lies, and these lies are destructive thoughts that obscure the nature of God, drawing us into agreement through sin. Demons seek always to destroy our destiny by separating us from the life of God and by usurping our authority on earth. This is the only purpose they have, temporary though it is.

Evil spirits certainly don't want to look at the reality of the Cross, which will ultimately sever their connection to humanity. They certainly don't want us to look at the reality of the Cross, which will ultimately bring us life. And yet, like angels, demons also do not force their way on us. When demons roam about, as the devil does looking for someone to devour, they look for something in us that is familiar to them. They are looking for a connection, a place to belong. They cannot rest where there is light; they move toward darkness. To find a place of comfort, they either have to attempt to usher darkness into a person through seduction, or find a place where it already is present.

We were created for relationship. Evil spirits take advantage of our nature by initiating relationships the same way they did in the Garden. They present to us a temptation characterized by deception, all for the purpose of gaining control. Our response to that deception gives demons access to us.

Just like Adam and Eve, we come into bondage based on our sinful responses to the empty promises. "Every one who commits sin is a slave to sin" (Jn 8:34). With every sin comes deception, and unconfessed sin leads to deeper bondage. Evil spirits bring increase to the original deception that we have embraced through sin. As deception deepens, we are increasingly blinded from the gift of turning to the Lord in repentance. Lies, now familiar to us, can appear like our friends; they become a source of comfort for us. Yet the lies bring death, and evil spirits are attracted to what is dead.

Like flies attracted to fresh manure, evil spirits appear instantaneously in the presence of sin. As they perceive rebellion of any sort, they come to bring greater destructive influence. They will bring thoughts such as self-justification, blame, excuses, bitterness, false judgments, destructive criticism, self-condemnation, or self-rejection to build a fortress around the foothold they have already gained.

Rather than attracting demons by making a place for the lie, let us invite angels to come to us. We cannot command them, but we can ask God to send angels, or we can attract them to us by focusing on God and the things of God. Angels are drawn toward us when we speak words that give life and encouragement. They are welcomed into our lives also as we recognize and honor these incredible beings that God has created for his purpose. As they come, angels will attend to us as bridesmaids attend to the bride. They will ready us for our union with God.

How Spirits Interact with the Soul

The *Catholic Encyclopedia* says:

> The soul may be defined as the ultimate internal principle by which we think, feel, and will, and by which our bodies are animated.[81]

Anyone having psychological training thinks in terms of helping a client work though issues about the way they think (about themselves, others, God), feel (what are the sources of disordered emotions such as resentment, bitterness, hopelessness, depression?), and express their will (in addictive behaviors, choices that are self-destructive). Those who have seen dramatic relief with their clients (or friends) through prayer for deliverance find it very natural to view the human person in terms of body, soul, and spirit, as found in Scripture:

> May the God of peace himself sanctify you wholly; and may your spirit and soul and body be kept sound and blameless at the coming of our Lord Jesus Christ.
>
> — 1 Thess 5:23

Based on this Scripture (and others — cf. Hebrews 4:12), as well as common experience, many Christians distinguish between the soul and the spirit. This enables them to explain that evil spirits can be present in the soul, entering the mind, binding the will, and manipulating the emotions, yet unable to touch the innermost depths of a person — his spirit. After all, if Satan, the father of lies, feeds us a deception, where does that lie go except into the mind, and thus into a person's soul? And yet the *Catechism* reminds us that St. Paul's distinction in 1 Thessalonians "does not introduce a duality into the soul" (*CCC* 367). Rather, "spirit" signifies that from creation, man is ordered to a supernatural end and that his soul can gratuitously be raised beyond all it deserves to communion with God (367). We must remember that the spirit, given by God at the moment of conception, is an integral dimension of the soul and cannot ever be separated from it. When the soul leaves the body upon death, it remains waiting to be reunited with the body at the resurrection of the dead. The spiritual soul, with its intellect, will, and emotions, will exist for eternity.

The *Catechism* refers to the soul as "the *spiritual principle* in man":

> In Sacred Scripture, the term "soul" often refers to human *life* or the entire human *person*. But "soul" also refers to the innermost aspect of man, that which is of greatest value in him, that by which he is most especially in God's image: "soul" signifies the *spiritual principle* in man.
>
> — *CCC* 363

Our entire being — body and soul, intellect, and will — is created for eternal life with God. Understanding the spiritual nature of our intellect and will is the first key to understanding how evil spirits interact with the soul.

Moral theologians have traditionally classified the work of the devil as temptation, obsession, and possession.[82] Temptation is, of course, every effort of the devil to seduce us to sin. Obsession (often used interchangeably with oppression) is the term used to describe the activity of the devil attacking and exerting influence on the individual from the outside. Fr. Wheeler uses the traditional understanding of obsession and oppression, but many in deliverance ministry now distinguish between the two — believing, as Fr. Scanlan and Randall Cirner do, that in obsession, the devil has access to the mind and will much like in possession, though in lesser degree.[83]

Christians who have sought deliverance prayer confirm this idea, often stating that they feel some "thing" leaving during prayer. They later report that they have been changed in deep ways that affected their minds, emotions, and wills. It is critical, however, to view the devil's work properly. When a person is obsessed or possessed, the devil acts from within, using the "external and internal senses"[84] to torment him and to manifest through him. But at no time does the devil ever reside in the soul of a believing Catholic. Exorcists writing about possession state clearly that in possession, a demon enters into a person's body but not his soul.[85]

The same is true for believers suffering from obsession. Though the devil clearly exerts influence from within, and though our spiritual faculties of intellect and will are affected, that effect happens only by indirect contact through some "bodily sense or faculty," as Balducci says. Along the continuum toward possession, this influence becomes stronger over time until the demonic spirit finally competes with the soul for control of the body.

In both the obsessed and possessed person, the soul is deeply wounded. We may picture the soul as a man, tied with cords around both wrists and ankles, unable to help himself. But if this wounded soul belongs to a believing Catholic who struggles against deep identification with sinful habits, there is healing and freedom to be had.

Understanding our freedom is the second aspect of understanding how spirits interact with our soul. We are created free and maintain that freedom, even though we are wounded by sin, overcome by deception, or tormented by the past, present, or future. In our wounding, we are like a town that has opened its doors to a usurping king or allowed the conquering barbarian to swarm over the walls. Pope John Paul II encourages us to defend our freedom as we wait for our "town's" liberation.

> Finally, Our Lady of Lourdes has a message for everyone. Be men and women of freedom! But remember: human freedom is a freedom wounded by sin. It is a freedom which itself needs to be set free. Christ is its liberator; he is the one who "for freedom has set us free" (cf. Gal. 5:1). Defend that freedom![86]

When Fr. Maximilian Kolbe was imprisoned in Auschwitz, he lost his outward freedoms, but he never lost his personal freedom to act in love. He expressed it by giving his life for another prisoner. We, too, are prisoners, captives to sin and unbelief, but we continue to have the freedom to choose to act in love. We are free to follow or to reject Christ. This freedom comes from God — who breathed into us a spirit, united to our intellect and will in our soul, when he created us. Although the gift of freedom can be compromised through sin, it cannot be entirely lost. We have "a freedom which itself needs to be set free," a freedom to defend.

Our true identity as children of God remains, even if obscured by sin. But then, if our very essence — our soul — is protected, how do evil spirits work to hold us in bondage and gain greater and greater influence over us?

The Role of Imagination in the Work of Evil Spirits

As mentioned previously, we need to remember that we are created in freedom for relationship. Evil spirits want to draw us into a relationship in which we yield our thoughts and our will to the promptings of God's enemy. Our yielding, our submission, our agreement is a free act.

According to St. Thomas Aquinas, the "Angelic Doctor," spirits influence us through the imagination by presenting thoughts and images to us.[87] Our encounter with images brings about an emotional response that sets the conditions for our thinking and choosing — but it doesn't completely determine our choices or how we choose to think about the images. We can always question our feelings; we can always decide what to do about them. So free will and the integrity of our reason are preserved.

For example, we might find a lustful image pleasurable — or we might be tormented by thoughts that remind us of past humiliation or cause us to worry about future failure. These images may be attractive or repulsive to us, depending on how we have learned to think. What kind of home have we made for impure thoughts? Do we encourage and feed thoughts of doom, or do we reject them, remembering instead the truth of God's love and plan for us? Do we welcome troubling thoughts by dwelling on them, aligning our thinking with that which is represented by the image in our minds, or do we turn from them and consider them in light of the truth that we have embraced in Jesus Christ?

Demons can present thoughts and images to our imaginations in an attractive way, and thereby lead us to dwell on evil. The more we allow the lies to settle, the more "tied up" our freedom becomes. We do not get into spiritual bondage the first time we receive a demonic inspiration and agree with it. Bondage takes place over time, as one thought builds on another. Since only God is omniscient — only God knows everything — we should not be deceived into thinking that evil spirits can read our thoughts. What they can do, however, is observe our lives, words, and actions; these reveal to them whether we have been receptive to their work as they have presented thoughts and images to us. If they observe actions or words that show a Christian's agreement with their deceptive thoughts, they will bombard the victim with images and thoughts that entangle him all the more in the deceptions to which he has already yielded.

People who have never established good interpersonal boundaries often have the same issues spiritually. The inability to distinguish between what comes through their imaginations and what comes from their own inner voice makes it difficult to know how to open and close the door of their "house" by firmly saying yes or no.

We can also reveal our thoughts to demons through our will, if we choose, by talking to them or focusing our thoughts toward them. Choosing to reveal our thoughts to them and seeking to receive information from them is very dangerous. This is like hanging a sign outside your home saying, "Demons Welcome Here!" We must fight for our freedom by retraining our imaginations — and by taking down every welcoming sign.

EXAMPLES OF SPIRITUAL BONDAGE

Typically, spiritual bondage is revealed in and through the personality. Personality can be defined as "the totality of somebody's attitudes, interests, behavioral patterns, emotional responses, social roles, and other individual traits that endure over long periods of time."[88] Over time, our response to either demonic or angelic inspiration will have its effect upon us and be manifest in our personality. Sacred Scripture calls these results either the "fruit of the Spirit" or the "works of the flesh." The bondage here is the agreement that we have given to the lie, the image, or the thought that is evil. The demons do not influence us from within the essence of who we are, but from without. I say it again: the prison in which our thoughts, our will, and our emotions rest is built by our agreement or submission to the lie, *not* by invasion or penetration of the soul.

Two illustrations will better explain the way we can be held in spiritual bondage. The first analogy shows how we can be in bondage through relationship.

Think of a seventeen-year-old young man and woman who have become consumed by their relationship with each other. Their emotions are telling them that they cannot live without each other; they both think, "I would rather die than have this relationship end." How did this happen?

First came physical and emotional attraction. Something inside them awakened, feeling the power of emotion and sexual desire at a depth never experienced before. This led to interaction, conversation, and communication. Soon they were secretly talking on the phone deep into the night. Socially, others began to relate to them as a couple — deepening the commitment they had already formed to their new joint identity. Their thinking about themselves and the future intermingled, and then this binding was consummated through sexual sin. In engaging sexually, each made a promise of the self to a relationship that lacked the foundation upon which to make such a commitment. Now, they are bound together before they've developed any meaningful ability to clearly know either their own thoughts or the true basis of a lifelong commitment.

Do these young people feel that they are free to choose another path? Probably not. Do they feel helpless, controlled, vulnerable, and fearful? Perhaps. Their growing sense of bondage, which feels real to them, came not from a complete loss of the internal freedom of the soul but from the increased wounding and compromised freedom caused by a codependent relationship.

Just so, our freedom is wounded as we yield ourselves to a relationship with deception. First, we entertain lies and false images in our minds; then, we believe our emotional response; and finally, we surrender our identity to a lie.

In the second analogy, a woman comes to the shelter for battered women. She has been there before. Her life is clearly in danger; the damage to her children appears to be irreversible — yet she goes back to the man who beats her. Is she free to decide not to? Yes. Is there a place within her that, by grace, she could draw on to make a different decision? Yes — she remains free. But fear of being on her own, of the unknown, of making her own decisions, or a whole host of other things holds her bound. These fears did not take hold in one day. They took hold through the series of decisions or non-decisions she made, building a whole way of thinking about herself that enslaves her to fear.

In like manner, our spiritual bondage does not spring up suddenly. We, too, make step-by-step agreements with evil, gradual decisions to fellowship with a lie. One day, we awaken and find that we are caught.

OVERCOMING THE WORK OF EVIL SPIRITS

The vast majority of the people for whom we pray gain freedom through identification of the lie, repentance, forgiveness, and renunciation. When the command is given, it is over, or new insight is given. Over the years I have often wondered if, in some cases, what we are casting out are really evil spirits or something else. Because they seemed too insignificant to be fallen angels, I have thought of them as lies that are spiritual, or as spirit-empowered lies.

With the help of Peter Kreeft's book, *Angels and Demons*, and my little knowledge of St. Thomas Aquinas, I now can see that my observations are reasonable. Spirits of hatred, lust, and rejection, for instance, are aspects of a spirit that becomes present to us though the focus of its thoughts (lies). Through our agreement with the lies, we become bound. It is our thoughts, agreeing with the spirit's lies, that create a binding. The intermingling of our thoughts (arising from the powers of our soul) and the enemies' lies establishes a relationship and a doorway for a spirit's presence. This will affect our emotions and lead to the compromising of our will. Over time, these bindings will become expressed in our personality.

But as we understand the dignity of our souls, recognize how demons interrelate with us, and learn about the freedom we have as sons and daughters of God, we will discover practical ways to disentangle from the presence of evil influence and find that the irrational fear and superstition surrounding the activities of evil spirits will be removed. In Christ, we are not helpless. United to Christ, as Pope Benedict XVI has told us, we have nothing to fear.

Acknowledgments

I am grateful to the many people who have made very important contributions to this book.

I thank Fr. Jeffrey Grob, who shared his doctoral thesis on exorcism with me and spent significant time responding to my thoughts and ideas about the relationship between deliverance and exorcism. His work was a starting place for my research, and he has made his thesis generously available to everyone at www.heartofthefather.com. I am grateful for his wisdom and kindness.

I also wish to thank Dr. Mary Healy, who came to my rescue during a final review of the book. I thank her for her expertise and for picking up many small but significant inconsistencies.

I thank Fr. Dennis J. Billy, CSsR, for advising me as I developed Appendix B.

I thank Ann Stevens, Philip Lozano, Fr. Michael Scanlan, TOR, and Fr. Francis Martin for reading portions of my work and giving me feedback.

I thank all those who read this book and took the time to write an endorsement.

I thank Priscilla Strapp for assisting in writing, organizing my material, and editing the manuscript.

I am grateful to Katherine Pugh for reviewing, editing, and generously giving her creative and theological insights.

I am grateful to Margaret Schlientz, PhD, who personally invited me in 2007 to attend a conference on deliverance and exorcism at Mundelein Seminary that was primarily directed to priests and bishops. This conference opened my eyes to the need for understanding non-confrontational deliverance in relationship to confrontational deliverance and exorcism.

I am especially grateful to those who shared their stories and allowed me to share them with you and to all those who through the years have asked questions about how the Unbound Model of deliverance fits into Catholic life.

Finally, I want to thank my wife, Janet, whose encouragement and steadfast love I depend on daily. I am especially thankful for her patience when I drifted away with ideas about what I was writing in the middle of dinner and other inappropriate times. Janet, my love, this book is dedicated to you.

About the Author

Neal Lozano holds a master's degree in religious education and has more than thirty-five years of pastoral experience helping people find freedom in Christ. As founders of Heart of the Father Ministries, Neal and his wife, Janet, travel both nationally and internationally, bringing the message of Unbound in training seminars and conferences.

In his book *Unbound: A Practical Guide to Deliverance*, Neal presents, in a very personal and instructive way, his approach to non-confrontational-style deliverance and healing that has been introduced and used around the world, in countries as far away as Ghana, Rwanda, and Papua New Guinea. To date, *Unbound* has been translated into Spanish, Ukrainian, Polish, Slovakian, and Slovenian, and soon will be in Russian.

Neal has also written the *Will You Bless Me?* series, comprised of three children's books. These tender stories speak to the hearts of parents and children alike, revealing the importance and power of the spoken blessing.

Neal and Janet have four grown sons and seven grandchildren.

For more information about *Unbound: Freedom in Christ* conferences or other resources, visit the Heart of the Father Ministries Web site, www.heartofthefather.com, or e-mail info@ heartofthefather.com.

Endnotes

1. See "Mental Health of College Students and Their Non-College-Attending Peers" by Carlos Blanco, MD, PhD, et al., *Archives of General Psychiatry* 2008; 65 (12): 1355, which detailed the results of the National Epidemiologic Study on Alcohol and Related Conditions.

2. BBC interview broadcast on WHYY, November 11, 2008.

3. Gabriel Amorth wrote *An Exorcist Tells His Story,* while Jose Antonio Fortea wrote *Interview with an Exorcist: An Insider's Look at the Devil, Demonic Possession, and the Path to Deliverance.*

4. Neal Lozano, *Unbound: A Practical Guide to Deliverance* (Grand Rapids, MI: Chosen Books, 2003).

5. Pope Paul VI, Address, *"Liberaci dal male,"* 15 November 1972, in *Insegnamenti di Paolo VI,* vol. 10, Vatican City, Tipografia poliglotta Vaticana, 1972, pp. 1168-1173, English translation in *The Pope Speaks,* 17 (1973), 315-319.

6. Joseph Ratzinger and Vittorio Messori, *The Ratzinger Report: an Exclusive Interview on the State of the Church,* trans. Salvator Attansio and Graham Harrison (San Francisco: Ignatius Press, 1985), 138.

7. Rev. Randall Foster, "Exorcism Course in Rome — An Article from Zenit," http://texanglican.blogspot.com/2005/09/exorcism-course-in-rome-article-from.html, Accessed December 4, 2008.

8. This is changing as a number of seminaries have begun to teach our future priests the basics of spiritual warfare. Mundelein Seminary in Chicago and Sacred Heart Major Seminary in Detroit are two where this is happening. Ralph Martin, the Director of Graduate Theology Programs in the New Evangelization at Sacred Heart, teaches that the ministry of Jesus in overcoming evil must continue in the Church today, not only in the official Rite of Exorcism, but in many other, easily accessible ways as well. In this program both Professor Martin and Dr. Mary Healy use my book *Unbound*

to supplement their own material. Besides teaching in his seminary classes, Martin has presented his thoughts to an audience of priests and seminarians at a conference at Mundelein and has published them under the title "The Authority of the Good Shepherd: Overcoming Evil" in the *Fifth Annual Symposium on the Spirituality and Identity of the Diocesan Priest: Good Shepherd — Living Christ's Own Pastoral Authority* (Omaha: Institute for Priestly Formation, 2006) pp. 69-81. Martin's article is also available as a free download at www.renewalministries.net.

9. L. Suenens, *Renewal and the Powers of Darkness,* trans. O. Prendergast (Ann Arbor, MI: Servant Books, 1983) 74. I am indebted to Fr. Jeffrey Grob, who quotes Cardinal Suenens in his doctoral dissertation, *A Major Revision of the Discipline on Exorcism: A Comparative Study of the Liturgical Laws in the 1614 and 1998 Rites of Exorcism* (St. Paul University, 2006), and concludes that Suenens' calls for both new pastoral teaching on exorcism and a revision of the criteria used to determine the authenticity of cases of possession have gone "largely unheeded." According to Grob, "To this day, no new pastoral document on exorcism has been issued and the revised rite includes exactly the same criteria — neither more nor less — than were first published in the rite of 1614. Both matters raised by Suenens deserve further consideration and discussion" (182).

10. Jeffrey S. Grob, *A Major Revision of the Discipline on Exorcism: A Comparative Study of the Liturgical Laws in the 1614 and 1998 Rites of Exorcism.* Dissertation submitted to the Faculty of Canon Law, St. Paul University, Ottawa, Canada, 5. See Appendix A for further distinctions regarding exorcism.

11. Irenaeus, *Against Heresies* II.32.4; http://www.newadvent.org/fathers/2802. htm, accessed 28 November, 2009.

12. Fr. Jose Antonio Fortea, *Interview with an Exorcist* (West Chester, PA: Ascension Press 2006), 72.

13. According to approved practice, the following are regarded as signs of demonic possession: extended utterance in an unknown tongue, or the ability to understand such utterance; the power to reveal what is distant and hidden; and the displaying of physical strength beyond what is appropriate to one's years, or natural state. These signs can offer some indication [of possession]. But since signs of this sort are not necessarily to be considered of devilish provenance, attention should be paid to other factors, especially in the realm of the moral and the spiritual, which can in a different way be evidence of diabolic intrusion. Examples of these are a violent aversion to God, the Most Holy Name of Jesus, the Blessed Virgin Mary and the Saints, the word of God, holy things, holy rites (especially of a sacramental nature) and holy images. And finally, careful consideration must be given to the manner in which all signs relate to faith and the spiritual struggle in the

Christian life; for indeed, the evil one is, above all, the enemy of God and of all that unites the faithful to the saving work of God. [Section 16. From a translation of the praenotanda from *De exorcismis et supplicationibus quibusdam (editio typica 1999),* rendered into English by Pierre Bellemare of St. Paul University.]

14. Gabriel Amorth, *An Exorcist Tells His Story* (San Francisco: Ignatius Press, 1999), 57.

15. Since exorcists do not usually speak about particular cases because of privacy issues, the wisdom that could be gained by taking a systematic look at what transpires in the person during the process of exorcism is often missing.

16. Some manuscripts read seventy-two.

17. Kilian McDonnell and George T. Montague, *Christian Initiation and baptism in the Holy Spirit, 1st amended ed.* (Collegeville, MN: Liturgical Press, 1991), 328-331.

18. Walter Bauer, *Orthodoxy and Heresy in Earliest Christianity* (Philadelphia: Fortress Press, 1971), 141.

19. Hans Von Campenhausen, *Ecclesiastical Authority and Spiritual Power in the Church of the First Three Centuries,* trans. J.A. Baker (Palo Alto, CA: Stanford University Press, 1969), 191.

20. Francis MacNutt, in his book *The Healing Reawakening: Reclaiming Our Lost Inheritance* (Grand Rapids, MI: Baker Books, 2006), traces the battle over the charism of healing in a similar way.

21. Von Campenhausen, 187.

22. Grob, 58.

23. *The Second Apology of St. Justin Martyr,* Chapter 6; http://www.newadvent. org/fathers/0127.htm. Accessed November 23, 2009.

24. The use of the word *deliverance,* as I am using it, is a recent development. In the late 1960s and 1970s, charismatic Catholics began driving out spirits in response to the fresh release of power that came with the baptism of the Holy Spirit. The words *deliverance* and *liberation* were commonly used among Pentecostals and charismatic Protestants at the time. Since the Church provided the Rite of Exorcism for the possessed, and since this rite was only to be used by a priest with the bishop's permission, a distinction between exorcism and deliverance was made to protect the faithful from confusion. This distinction has been widely accepted throughout the Church.

25. Here, Grob cites R.J.S. Barrett-Lennard, *Christian Healing After the New Testament* (Lanham, MD: Rowman and Littlefield, 1994), 202.

26. Grob, 55, 59.

27. *Origen Against Celsus: Book VII,* Roberts-Donaldson English Translation,

Chapter IV; http://www.earlychristianwritings.com/origen.html. Accessed November 23, 2009.

28. Benedict XVI, address to bishops and representatives of ecclesial movements and new communities, May 17, 2008.

29. Benedict XVI, *Jesus of Nazareth* (New York: Doubleday, 2007), 56-57.

30. Acts 10:38 " . . . how God anointed Jesus of Nazareth with the Holy Spirit and with power; how he went about doing good and healing all that were oppressed by the devil, for God was with him."

31. Vine, W.E., *Expository Dictionary of Old and New Testament Words* (Grand Rapids, MI: Fleming H. Revell, 1981).

32. Luke 8:26-38.

33. An old Pentecostal minister once told me that a sign of a Holy Ghost church was that the demonized would come to the services, often not knowing how they got there or why they came to that particular church. This was puzzling. Why would those controlled by demons be able to come? The answer is that while they may seem to be controlled, there is a part of them that is very aware of what will torment the demons because it also torments them. These poor folk find their way to the church, despite their own torment, so they can have their enemies tormented and driven out.

34. See Daniel 10, where the angel prince of the kingdom of Persia resists the archangel Michael for twenty-one days.

35. Pope Paul VI, in his apostolic exhortation *Evangelii Nuntiandi*, states: "We wish to confirm once more that the task of evangelizing all people constitutes the essential mission of the Church. It is a task and mission which the vast and profound changes of present day society make all the more urgent. Evangelizing is in fact the grace and vocation proper to the Church, her deepest identity. She exists in order to evangelize." *On Evangelization in the Modern World*, December 8,1975, www.vatican.va/holy_father/paul_vi/apost_exhortations/documents/hf_p-vi_exh_19751208_evangelii-nuntiandi_en.html; accessed January 28, 2009; 14.

36. http://www.timesonline.co.uk/tol/news/world/europe/artciel3981337.ece.

37. George Thomas, "Is the Devil Gaining a Foothold in Rome?" January 1, 2009; http://www.cbn.com/cbnnews/360212.aspx; accessed January 22, 2009.

38. Gabriel Amorth, " 'The Smoke of Satan in the House of the Lord,' The Reform of the Rite of Exorcism." *30 Days*, June 2000.

39. Fr. Rufus Pereira believes this problem is spread across the worldwide Church. He says: "There is not a single exorcist appointed in most countries, and even in most dioceses in many of the other countries, and so our people

in their need have no alternative but to go either to spiritists or to neo-pentecostal healers. Fortunately, the Catholic Charismatic Renewal has stepped in the gap in this spiritual warfare through a renewed ministry of deliverance, one of its greatest contributions to the Catholic Church today. Far from competing with the official ministry of Exorcism, this ministry rather complements and supports it, as many exorcists have told me personally." "Exorcism and Deliverance for Healing, Reconciliation and New Life," *Prayer for Healing* (Rome, ICCRS, 2003), 242.

40. Grob, 17.

41. Fr. Martin stated this publicly at Mundelein Seminary and confirmed it through personal correspondence, in which he wrote: "When asked by Fr. Rufus Pereira concerning the third paragraph of Statement of the Congregation of the Doctrine of the Faith, September 19, 1984, the then Cardinal Prefect of the Congregation, Cardinal Joseph Ratzinger, replied that the restriction applied to public assemblies. This is clear from the Latin word *conventus*, used to designate the nature of the assembly being considered."

42. McManus, Fr. James, CSsR, in *Deliverance Prayer*, Matthew Linn and Dennis Linn, eds. (Mahwah, NJ: Paulist Press, 1981), 246. Emphasis mine.

43. See Appendix A for a detailed explanation of the controversy over exorcism and deliverance in the Church.

44. Pope John Paul II, quoted in an interview with Fr. Amorth, "The Reform of the Rite of Exorcism." *30 Days,* June 2000.

45. Pope Benedict XVI, "On Christ as Head," General Audience, January 14, 2009; http://zenit.org/article-24784?l=english; accessed January 22, 2009.

46. Fr. James Wheeler, SSJ, "Deliverance Within the Total Ministry of the Church" (*Deliverance Prayer*, 183). Fr. Wheeler's categories are very helpful from a practical and pastoral perspective. There is a great need to recognize the lower levels of demonic influence working though negative emotions and controlling relationships. The traditional three categories of temptation, obsession, and possession may not fully explain the full spectrum of demonic influence. Francis MacNutt goes further than Wheeler and distinguishes between oppression and obsession as well. He points out that oppression comes from the Latin verb meaning "to press down upon." Pressing down is activity from the outside, not the inside. Many authors now use the four terms to describe demonic activity.

47. Wheeler, 186.

48. Ibid., 185.

49. Ibid., 185.

50. Ibid., 189.

51. See Appendix B for a fuller explanation of the Church's teaching on spirits — both angels and demons — and how they interact with the soul.

52. Manifestations are involuntary physical reactions such as shouts, twisting of the face, blacking out, and so on. When an individual renounces his yielding to a particular evil spirit, the body may visibly reveal that demonic force.

53. Many books and articles are written on angels and demons. Some suggest that what we are dealing with are aspects of fallen angels. For example, captivity to bitterness or hatred may be one touch of part of a demon's personality. Others look to Genesis 6:2, where we are told that the sons of God intermarried with daughters of men, to support the idea that there are other spirits besides fallen angels that are part of the demonic kingdom. There is much we do not understand, but this much is clear: St. Paul cautions us against being too concerned with "myths" and "opposing ideas of what is falsely called knowledge" (1 Tim 1:4, 6:20), and encourages us instead to "put to death" negative emotions and to "clothe yourselves" instead with the fruit of his Spirit (Col 3: 5-17), teaching believers in our care how to lead holy lives (Titus 2). The teachings of Unbound seek to help believers follow Paul's encouragement.

54. Wheeler, 197.

55. Ibid., 200.

56. Pope Benedict XVI, *Jesus of Nazareth*, 47.

57. Pope John Paul II, encyclical letter *Redemptoris Missio* (1990), 46.

58. This is consistent with the Catholic understanding of anthropology, that all humans (created in the image of the Trinity) are relational by design.

59. When they do not see transformation, many priests believe that the penitents are benefiting from receiving the grace of the sacrament anyway and would never judge how God may be using the grace in a person's life. The priest is the servant of God's grace and mercy. Most priests would never discourage anyone from availing him or herself of the grace of the sacrament. But recognizing that the person may be receiving the grace in a limited way, they would seek to give spiritual direction to help the person make a turn toward a deeper spiritual life.

60. Andrew M. Brown, "You can't talk to young people about salvation. What does that mean to them?" December 19, 2008; http://www.catholicherald.co.uk/features/f0000353.shtml; accessed January 25, 2009.

61. Post-Synodal Apostolic Exhortation *Ecclesia in Africa*, September 14, 1995. http://www.vatican.va/holy_father/john_paul_ii/apost_exhortations/documents/hf_jp-ii_exh_14091995_ecclesia-in-africa_en.html, 73.

62. *Redemptoris Missio*, 78.

63. Benedict XVI, General Audience, January 25, 2009. www.zenit.org/article-24905?/=english; accessed February 2, 2009.

64. *Jesus of Nazareth*, 62.

65. Ibid., 60

66. Ibid., 60.

67. *Redemptoris Missio,* 14. Emphasis mine.

68. Ibid., 16.

69. Tertullian, *De Spectaculis,* trans. by the Rev. S. Thelwall as *The Shows, Chapter XXIX.* http://www.earlychristianwritings.com/tertullian.html; accessed November 20, 2009.

70. Cf. Matthew 26:63; Mark 5:7; Acts 19:13. Note, however, that none of these texts portrays a proper use of adjuration.

71. Congregation for the Doctrine of the Faith, *Inde ab aliquot annis,* September 29, 1985, in *AAS,* 77 (1985), 1169-1170. English translation in *Canon Law Digest,* vol. 11, 276-277. A copy in Latin can be found at www.ewtn.com/ library/CURIA/CDFEXORC.htm.

72. See footnote 40 in chapter 6 above.

73. Some argue that this restriction, too, applies only to public ministry.

74. Quoted by Robert Moynihan in his editorial in *Inside the Vatican*, February 2006.

75. Although the "Long Ending" of Mark (Mk 16:9-20) is not present in some ancient manuscripts of the Gospel, and most scholars believe it was added by a later scribe, the Church still considers this section to be part of the inspired and canonical Gospel.

76. Grob, 5. As noted above, however, to avoid confusion in this book I reserve the term "exorcism" for public exorcism and use the term "deliverance" for what Grob calls a private exorcism.

77. St. Cyprian, *Letter* 70, 15.2. *The Letters of St. Cyprian of Carthage,* Vol. 4, trans. G.W. Clarke (New York, NY: Newman Press, 1984) 44.

78. Ibid.

79. Thomas Aquinas, *Summa Theologica* I, 114.3.

80. The free will of angels is different from the free will of fallen humanity. Angels have made a fundamental choice, similar to the choice that we will make throughout our lifetime. The ultimate choice angels have made for God is irreversible. They no longer can choose to do evil. However, they remain free to choose the good that is before them and may respond to our prayers within the context of the will of God, to which they have fully surrendered.

81. *Catholic Encyclopedia,* www.catholic.org/encyclopedia. Accessed March 11, 2009.

82. See Tanquerey, Adolphe, *The Spiritual Life: A Treatise on Ascetical and Mystical Theology* (*2nd & revised ed.*), trans. Herman Branderis (Tournai, Belgium: Desclee & Co., 1930).

83. Michael Scanlan and Randall Cirner (*Deliverance from Evil Spirits*; Ann Arbor, MI: St. Anthony's Messenger Press, 1980) distinguish between obsession and oppression, saying that obsession is the work of evil spirits holding the person in bondage from within, while oppression is the influence of evil spirits from without, bringing feelings of heaviness or discouragement. While others use various words to describe these realities, I have found this distinction very helpful for practical ministry.

84. Corrado Balducci, *The Devil*, translated and adapted by Jordan Aumann (New York: Alba House, 1990), 95.

85. Fr. Jose Antonio Fortea answers the question "What is demonic possession?" He writes: "Demonic possession is the phenomenon in which a demon resides in the body of a human being. At specific moments, the demon can speak and move through it without the person being able to prevent this. Only the body is susceptible to demonic possession. A demon does not reside in or in any way "possess" the soul of the person. In all circumstances, the soul continues to be free and incapable of being possessed. *Interview with an Exorcist* (West Chester, PA: Ascension Press, 2006), 72. Balducci agrees, saying "As regards the influence of the devil on human beings . . . he can have direct and immediate contact only with what is corporeal, namely, the human body and its organs and functions. . . . He cannot, however, touch the purely spiritual faculties of intellect and will, except indirectly through some bodily sense or faculty." (95)

86. From the homily of John Paul II, Apostolic pilgrimage to Lourdes, Sunday, August 15, 2004; http://www.vatican.va/holy_father/john_paul_ii/homilies/2004/documents/hf_jp-ii_hom_20040815_lourdes_en.html, accessed December 8, 2009.

87. For further discussion of the ways spirits influence the imagination, see Thomas Aquinas, *Summa Theologica* I, Question 111.

88. Encarta Dictionary.